High Tea

High Tea

K. Cimone

Khia Moon Smith

Copyright © 2022 by K. Cimone

All rights reserved. No part of this book may be reproduced in any manner whatsoever without written permission except in the case of brief quotations embodied in critical articles and reviews.

First Printing, 2022

Leila, Micah, and Mason
My heartbeats outside of my chest.
My reasons.
My why.
My loves.

Everything I do is for you. You are my motivation and my fuel.
You keep me going.
I love you forever and always, times infinity.

CONTENTS

DEDICATION v

INTRODUCTION

1. THE MOTHER LOAD — 3
2. HOUSTON BOUND...AND UNBOUND — 8
3. SIS, PUT DOWN THE KOOL-AID! — 13
4. BAA, BAA, BLACK SHEEP — 19
5. 2002 — 22
6. 2003 — 26
7. GUARD YOUR GRILL, GIRL! — 32
8. SECRETS AND LIES — 39
9. THE CROWN LIFE — 44
10. I...DO? — 51
11. "P" IS FOR PEDOPHILE — 58

CONTENTS

12 | LIFE 66

13 | I CHOOSE ME 84

ACKNOWLEDGEMENTS

INTRODUCTION

To know me is to love me, and that means ALL of me—including this chip on my shoulder that I so begrudgingly refer to as "Bebe." Our relationship isn't the best—actually, it's the worst! This chip isn't one that I would tag as a grudge or a grievance. Its more along the lines of disappointment that has slowly morphed into a chip of disdain—all due to her behavior over the years.

If you haven't guessed it by now, Bebe is my mother. She and I didn't have a relationship as I was going through my formative years. As I grew older, the decline grew even more steep. Now, in adulthood, I'm able to see just how much of a negative impact she has had in my decisions and in my life in general. I'm not saying that I blame her for everything bad that has happened to me...but I am saying that I do blame her for a good bit of it. Not to say that I don't take ownership for my own personal decisions in life—because I most definitely do. I'm a firm believer that there is always a root cause for a person's actions. That cause doesn't excuse a person from the consequences of their choices, but it most definitely can be an influence or the reason for their decision to take said action. Learning the root cause can shed light and help immensely in fixing whatever unacknowledged problems there may be.

People that only know *of* me or who just may not be *that* close to me usually think of me as harsh, somewhat brash when it comes to the subject of my maternal unit. I'm often seen as super protective and overanalytical. But again, to truly know me and my why is to know *everything*, and up until now, that just wasn't something that I was ready to let everyone in on--including those who I have been good friends with for years. Letting everyone in on this aspect of my life has been a bit taboo for me. Really, there are only five people in what I like to refer to as my "inner circle" who had any glimpse of the tragedy that is my familial life...and even they were shielded from a lot of the madness. Until now.

I don't know if it was a subconscious fear of judgement, of ridicule, or just plain old embarrassment, but it wasn't until just recently that I've gotten to the point of not really caring anymore about whatever people decide to rush to. Either way, it's time to let go of all of this baggage I've been carrying around for decades in the form of a façade, and spill the tea. I've been screaming and preaching about self-care, and here I am dragging such heavy weights behind me in an attempt to protect others—others who didn't give a damn about protecting me and mine. This project has been my own private therapy session. It has allowed me to let go of what I've kept locked away for so long, and step into the sunlight. Welcome to my mental and emotional enema.

1

THE MOTHER LOAD

"It's all about finding the calm in the chaos"
-Donna Karan

Alright, so from the top, here it goes…a little history/background on the reason—well, part of the reason—I am the way that I am. Let me start by saying that my relationship with my maternal unit hasn't always been as sour as it is today. It truly has been an accumulation of events over the years that has taken us to this place. With each mishap, poor decision, argument, etc., I lost more and more patience and sympathy for this woman.

My maternal unit had me when she was 20yrs old. She was a single mother—but not in the way that we see and view single mothers as nowadays. My biological dad was definitely not the absentee type. He was very much present and still is to this day. In fact, our relationship grew stronger and stronger as I got older, and she got out of the way. But back when I was younger, he was as only as involved as she would allow him to be. Yeah, one of those baby mamas.

I remember one time—I had to be about four—I was with my dad and went to visit his side of the family. I was at my Granny's, where two of my aunts also lived—one of them was just a teenager still. I spent the night with them which was always so much fun. To everyone, I was like their own little baby doll. Well, with this particular visit, while I was at my Granny's, it began to rain so hard that it flooded badly, and fast. I remember this also happened to be around the time that my dad was supposed to take me back home. Well, the apartment complex that my Granny lived in and the roads around it were completely flooded and impassable, and there was no chance my dad's Corvette was going to make it through the water. So, he wrapped be back up in his giant raincoat so I wouldn't get soaked and we ran back upstairs to my Granny's apartment and called my maternal unit. The telephone conversation that took place between the two of them, and then with myself, was when I got my first taste of just how irrational and how much of a pill this woman was. While I don't remember our conversation verbatim, I do remember her saying that I wasn't going back ever again. I remember hearing my dad's end of the conversation and him trying to explain that he couldn't drive through the flood waters and that it wasn't safe. Whatever else was said between her and my dad must have been something horrible because the next thing that I can definitely recall was one of my aunts pulling me into her room and walk-in closet (she had soooo many of the most beautiful clothes!) and with tears in her eyes, telling me how much she loved me and if we were never able to see each other again, that she wanted me to know that I would always be her baby and that she would always love me no matter what. This whole incident was a lot to try and process—especially at my young age.

Fast forward to the time where I'm about 5yrs old. By this time, she had now been married for maybe two years to her first husband—who to this day, I still adore as a second father. I consider him as much my father as my biological dad. He was already playing the stepdad role, but he stepped up and filled in extra during the times the maternal unit would push my biological father away. Of course, she doesn't get along great with my stepdad at all anymore. But that's her pattern—anyone who makes sense and calls her out on her crap becomes an enemy. Go figure. Anyhow...

Now, we are living in California and I'm a big sister to my little brother, who is about five and a half years my junior. I loved living our lives in California. I can still remember exactly where we lived and places we would frequent (thanks Google Maps!). This is where a lot of my friendships and memories were made. It's just that some of them were sprinkled with not so hot memories and questionable friendships. How so, you ask? Well, buckle up…

Take this lady named Marilyn. She was a neighbor that lived in an upstairs unit across the courtyard from our unit. I haven't the slightest idea what Bebe was thinking with what she allowed to happen with this lady. In hindsight, Marilyn was definitely an unstable character. I remember her being super nice and imaginative—but now I know that at minimum, she was dealing with some unchecked battles mentally and/or emotionally. She had to be in her mid-50s, and she lived alone…with a house full of dolls and bears. Can we say creepy?! She would invite me over to play dress up and have tea parties with her in her apartment—and Bebe would allow it! I remember times when she would stand on her part of the balcony outside of her apartment—wrapped in nothing but a bedsheet fashioned into something like a tube dress—and nothing else. With her tube-sheet dresses and off the wall makeup, she would yell across the courtyard asking if I could come over and play. Nope, that's not weird at all, right? I never wanted to go over there, but at the urging of Bebe, I would "just go and keep her company for a bit." Again, in hindsight, I begin to wonder if those times away were the times that Bebe had the opportunity to get high without me interrupting. Pure speculation, but not an outlandish accusation, as she admittedly had a drug problem back when I was younger.

As a kid, walking into her bedroom without knocking once and catching my mother and one of her girlfriends—who she later in life confirmed was in fact always coked up—putting stuff in their faces and getting into such an uproar about my intrusion, I didn't know to put two and two together. As an adult, now I know. As an adult, I can see why you would be okay with allowing your child to go "play" unsupervised with the cuckoo lady across the courtyard. As an adult, I can see why going next door to hang out with the self-proclaimed Romani lady and her abusive adult son and younger daughter was cool. I can also understand now why my friend Margaret and her sweet Korean family that lived just a couple of doors down were okay with me playing with their daughter *outside*, but I wasn't allowed to step foot past their doorway. I can put these instances together and see that this had to be the only reason why a "parent" (and I use that term loosely, here) would make such off the wall decisions and allowances regarding their child. Here is where I begin to question her thought processes, actions, and decisions.

By the time I was about 9yrs old, Bebe had soured things with my stepdad, and they separated. I was pissed about it, but I would never act out. We were living in a townhouse/condo complex during this time—myself, my little brother, and now 1yr old little sister—and she began dating this guy named Rod. I did not like him. At all. I doubt she knows this, but to this day, I resent the fact that she and my stepdad divorced...and this Rod character took that resentment to astronomical heights. He basically moved in and tried his best to get on our "good side," but I was fully aware of his bullshit façade. He had a temperament that I did not care for one bit.

To get away from the newfound chaos that was our home, I found escape in spending time with the landlord's kids. They had a big family—six kids total—and they welcomed me with open arms as one of their own. It was so much fun over there. Their youngest daughter took me under her wings—she was maybe six years older than me, and the big sister I'd always wanted. We did everything...played in her older sisters' clothes and makeup, tortured her younger brother, sleepovers...it was everything to me! There were times I would just go over to their unit just to be away from my own house. To add to my joy, her mother and father were a set of parents that was a welcome change of scenery compared to what I had been seeing over the past few months. I spent time in the kitchen learning how to make tamales and sopapilla and was the bonus kid of the family during their family monopoly nights. Bebe decided that she was done being abused by Rod. She aborted his baby and decided that it was time to move back home to Houston. It felt like she was tearing my family apart. Again.

2

HOUSTON BOUND...AND UNBOUND

"When all you know is fight or flight, red flags and butterflies all feel the same"
-Cindy Cherie

In late 1992, we migrated back to our hometown of Houston. Bebe loaded us up on a Greyhound bus and we traveled from Southern California to Houston, TX. Let me tell you this...because of this particular bus ride, I will never ever EVER take a Greyhound bus to any location. Ever. First of all, why in God's name would you, a young single woman juggling three young kids and luggage, think that it's a good idea to take a bus by yourself across three states? It's not like we were in any danger when we left California. She just never thinks things through. We were literally walking targets for any child snatcher. Thank God for protecting babies and fools! Second, there was the pregnant lady that was on our bus for a majority of the trip made me want to vomit on one too many occasions. Instead of holding on until we got to one of the many rest stops we took, this chick would take a dump in the bus port-o-potty and man...that smell is something that I will probably never forget.

We moved in with my aunt and her two kids—the youngest of which I was close to. All of us crammed into a trailer. My cousin is the youngest of two, with her older brother being much older than her...so it was almost like she was an only child until I came around. We are only five months apart, so naturally we would gravitate to each other. We shared a room, went to the same school, and shared the same friends. We even dressed alike. We bonded fast and did just about everything together like we were meant to be twins. We each were the sister that the other didn't have but needed badly. We attended Gregg Elementary School, which was right around the corner from the middle school where my aunt worked as a cafeteria manager. She once worked as the manager at Gregg, so for us, that meant we got perks! Since she had to be to work at the middle school earlier than our elementary school opened, we were allowed to hang out in the cafeteria with the other workers that used to work under my aunt. These ladies would spoil us with early morning sweets and snacks and extra breakfasts. At our age, that was a flex. Attending Gregg was completely different from the school I attended in California. Gregg was in a predominantly black area. Both the Principal and Vice Principal were African American, as were a good chunk of the teachers and staff--a total shift from the predominantly white school I spent the first five years of my schooling years in. At Gregg, we sang the "Lift Every Voice And Sing" (the Black National Anthem) immediately after the Pledge of Allegiance each day. Gregg was also unique in that it still offered the paddle as a form of punishment during school hours. At the beginning of the school year, parents signed a permission slip either declining or allowing the use of the paddle. Let me tell you...this is not something you wanted, at all! If you were one of the unlucky ones to earn your turn at the paddle, you were either going to get it from the Vice Principal, or the cowboy boot, cowboy hat, and big Texas belt buckle wearing Principal, Mr. Harris. Luckily (well, not really), all of my whoopings took place at home.

    My cousin introduced me to her best friend and her sisters that lived across the street. Once again, I had playdates and sleepovers to escape to—a welcomed getaway from the times Bebe had her boyfriend over to visit. We would spend hours and hours riding bikes around the trailer park, catching crawfish in the bayou, and kicking over gigantic ant beds in the grass. We played in the heat, the sun, and the rain. Trust me, anything was better than sitting in front of the TV and pretending that you don't notice the trailer rocking or hearing the headboard in the bedroom rhythmically bumping up against the wall while the song "Knocking Boots" played loudly in the background—in a failed attempt to try and drown out moans. She seriously should have thought her camouflage attempts out a little better—so that her 10yr old daughter wouldn't have to be introduced to sex in that manner. It probably would have kept her daughter's curiosity from peaking at such a young age. I personally don't think that a 10yr old should be experimenting with and performing explicit activities with the same sex (or even the opposite). But hey, it happened, and she wasn't the least bit concerned. It wasn't her priority. Turns out, Mr. Knocking Boots wasn't going anywhere anytime soon. John would end up becoming stepdad number two. Yay [insert sarcasm here]. February 1994 would usher in nuptials that would forever change our family dynamic...and not for the better.

Ever since the first day I met him, John—husband #2—didn't sit well with me. At just 10yrs old I didn't quite know what intuition was, but the gut feeling that I've carried over all these years...I would later learn exactly what it meant, and I would learn the hard way. First of all, this guy is only thirteen years older than me. I would never come to fully respect him as a parent. Bebe wanted me to view this person who was young enough to be my big brother as my *stepdad*. Add to that all of the bad feelings I had about him...not happening! And as if I didn't care for him enough, John was in the Navy and had orders to move to Virginia. Once again, just two months after they wed and barely a year after us moving back to Houston, she was tearing me away from everything that made me happy.

In April of 1994, we loaded up a moving truck with the furniture we had. It was one of those moving trucks that had an opening between the front cab and the back storage area. They pushed a mattress up against the opening in the truck and loaded the rest of the big furniture up against it so that me, my 5yr old little brother, and 2yr old little sister had somewhere to hang out while they drove during the 24-hour road trip to our new home in Virginia Beach. Did you catch that? Three kids riding around on a mattress, UNRESTRAINED, in the back of a box truck. Talk about ensuring safety!

We landed in Virginia Beach, VA, right at the oceanfront. Our first month or so was lived out in an Econo Lodge down on the resort strip while my parents searched for a more permanent residence. By this time, I was in the 5th grade and beginning to be a bit self-conscious about things...mainly having to tell new friends I made that we were living out of a hotel. It was embarrassing, but it was what it was. Not embarrassing because I was vain, but because this age group can have the tendency to be classist. Pre-teen middle schoolers are brutal! Thankfully though, it wasn't for too long. We soon moved over into the Magic Hollow area on a street named Blackstone Court. Here, I made friends with neighbors who were also my new classmates at Plaza Middle School. I loved being at school and outside with friends and finally being able to be free again and escape the jail cell called home. I would skate, ride bikes, swing and hang off trees, hang out at the park and basketball court at the end of the street...you name it, we did it! There was even a neighbor who grew honeysuckle, blackberries, and raspberries. She would let us just play and pick fruit all day long. There was no need to go inside for snacks and lunch. I loved being there. Being around my peers. My escape.

As usual, once I found solace, it was time to uproot and move on. We lived on Blackstone Court for hardly a year before we up and moved to an apartment and townhome complex closer to his naval base. Goodbye friends. Goodbye school. Hello new everything. I began 7th grade in a new home and a new middle school--Virginia Beach Middle School.

We would only live in the complex for eight months before we would move into military housing. Lucky for me, the new military housing was in the same school district...so that was one less move to deal with. If you've been keeping up, we are at a total of five moves in just three years. Talk about stability...

Our new housing situation was finally stable. We would end up living in military housing until about 2002. It was here, in Wadsworth, that I was finally able to settle, be comfortable, and make lifelong friends. I became fast friends with our next-door neighbors' daughter, Jessica. We both came from families where we were older than a bunch of our siblings, so our times away was golden. Malls, movies, walks, and even just hanging out with the other neighborhood kids...this was our freedom. It was in Wadsworth where I had my first crush, first boyfriend, and first kiss--both of those last two being top secret, of course. There were so many memories and friendships forged here that I cherish to this day.

3

SIS, PUT DOWN THE KOOL-AID!

*"The prophets prophesy falsely,
And the priests rule on their own authority;
And My people love it so!
But what will you do at the end of it?"*
-Jeremiah 5:31

When we moved to Virginia Beach in 1994, church was just something that me and my family went to every once in a while. It wasn't the foundation of our family at all. Don't get me wrong—we weren't anti-God or anything, but we also weren't super spiritual either. We were best described as "valuing the commandments and following The Golden Rule."

We visited quite a few churches before we found one, we thought was going to be our home church. Our family was invited to attend service at a church called Redemptive Life Christian Fellowship. It was a smaller congregation...maybe only about 20 people max. The pastor and his wife were quite charming. They had no children of their own but seemed to welcome all of the church members children with open arms. When we first began attending the church, it was being held in their neighborhood community clubhouse. Back home in Houston, when I attended our family church, it was a traditional looking church...so this idea of a non-traditional building really felt odd to me. Even more odd was when the pastors announced that they finally had a building of their own—a storefront location.

Words cannot express how uncomfortable I was going to a storefront church sandwiched between a hair salon and print shop. My parents would always want to invite my friends to visit church. I would just drop my head in shame to myself when they would agree to come. By this time, the embarrassment wasn't because of the building they chose to worship in—don't get me wrong. I still felt odd—but because of the relationships that had morphed over the years of attending and being under the spiritual guidance of the pastors. Like I said, in the beginning the pastors were so very warm and welcoming to me and the other youth/kids of the congregation.

As the years passed, and I grew older, tension began to develop between myself and my parents. This tension was aggravated even more by the pastor's wife—a self-proclaimed prophetess. Every Sunday she had something new to tell my mother. A message. A message about things that I did wrong. After every church service, we'd stand in line to greet our leaders...but to me, I was standing in line to endure this week's condemnation and accusations. There were sometimes where I was surprised with just a big hug—followed by the strong scent of the prophetess' Dune perfume seeping into my clothing. A day long reminder of all the ways that I've "sinned" during the week. It was those surprises—that of just a hug, sans condemnation, that I hoped and prayed for whenever my friends would agree to visit one of the services. To this day, I wonder who she was getting her "messages" from. Either her cords were tangled, or she was listening to the wrong entity.

I can recall one Christmas while we were members of the church, that the "prophetess" accused me of some type of sin of sorts. She then—in concert with my parents, decided that the best punishment would be for me not to open my Christmas gifts with everyone else on Christmas day. So, the next morning...right on schedule...we were all awakened to gather around the tree and say a prayer (like we always did before opening gifts). Then came both the excitement and the sadness. I sat on the couch and watched my parents, and my siblings open all of their gifts with excitement, I wouldn't even be allowed to touch a gift for an entire week. I was 13 or 14 at the time.

I endured all types of accusations from having sex with guys to having a crush on my stepfather. Yes, you read that right. She even told my mother to watch me because I had the hots for my stepfather and that I often flirted with him. Little does the "prophetess" know she had THAT message totally backwards...but we'll cover that one in another chapter. In all honesty, I believe that this was that pivotal moment in our relationship where me and my mother began rolling downhill with no brakes. Oftentimes, it felt like I couldn't do anything right to her. There was never any acceptance of me. I had always envied my friends and their relationships with their parents. I blamed the "prophetess" for contributing to our lack thereof.

In 1999, while we were members of this cult—I mean, church—there was a lady that my parents took in and later befriended. She had two little toddler boys and was recovering from drug addiction. She wanted to begin going to church and living a Christina life. Of course, the only righteous option was for her to attend our home church. And so, it was...her family was added to the roster. A few months after we took her in, we learned that she was pregnant. After she had her baby—a beautiful little girl—she had to deal with some legal matters that had been pending for some time. As it turns out, she would have to go to jail and her children would go into foster care if they couldn't be placed with family.

The boys would end up going with family, and her baby girl—whom I had become insanely attached to—would stay with us. And by us, I mean me. While my parents volunteered to keep the baby to help out, it was me who would shoulder the responsibility of caring for her. I was 16yrs old, in high school, an athlete, with a job, and now taking care of an infant. Food, diapers, clothes, etc..... it all came out of my paycheck. My parents were more like babysitters when it came to her. My weekday routine went a little something like this:

- Up around 5:30am to prep for the day and school
- Get the baby fed and put back down to sleep...hand off to Bebe
- *School & track practice – 6:30a – 4p*
- Home and baby duties continue
- Try to get some homework done
- Playtime, bath, dinner
- Baby down to sleep
- Finish up homework between feedings

She would end up staying with us for almost three years—until just after I graduated high school and moved out into my own place. Here I was...living the life of a teen mom. Do I regret it? No. Am I resentful for having to take on such a great responsibility? Absolutely not. I am grateful that I was there to teach her the things she needed. I am grateful that I could provide for her, and that she was able to grow up in a stable, loving, and nurturing environment.

When my senior year of high school rolled around in 2000-2001, things finally began to look a little but 'up' for me. I began dating this guy—we'll call him "D." He and his family came from a Christian background just like mine, they attended a large church in the area – CRC. When D and I decided to really be exclusive, we agreed it was time for our families to meet. He had a large family that was very loving and welcoming of both myself and my family. Then, while in the middle of their meet and greet, the best thing ever happened...D's mom invited me to go to church with them one week. I know, I know...how's a church invite the best thing ever? With the family I had if you didn't go to church you were going to hell. So, this was the ultimate level of acceptance. Of course, my parents offered to have D join us as well. I cringed as usual. Everything worked out great though. D's church had an early service that was over and done with in enough time for me to still make it to my family's church service—because yes, I still had to go with my own family.

When I first visited, I was in awe. This is the way that I remembered church. They had a choir, we weren't in church from 9am to 3pm, and most noticeable...the sermons that were preached weren't all condemnation and full of Greek translations that left us in a state of confusion for half a service They were down to earth messages of love, hope, and clear teachings of the bible. I was hooked. I wanted my entire family to get out of what—to me—felt borderline cult-like. Finally, after much pleading and convincing, my family decided to visit. During the service, I could see it in their eyes. They noticed the differences. The atmosphere. This was the moment that they finally realized that what they subjected us to, was not healthy. It wasn't Christ-centered. It wasn't love.

Needless to say, the "prophetess" wasn't happy about this visit. AT ALL. She would be even more pressed when we as a family decided to make this place our new church home. And when I say pressed, I mean PRESSED! When my parents decided it was time to leave the compound, they had to attend a meeting with the pastors...and the whole church! Picture an intervention hosted by the pastors, with church members as participants, and things getting borderline physical. Yeah, it went there. From what I understand, there were even physical attempts to keep them from leaving the building. While I didn't witness this myself, I don't think it far from them to resort to such tactics.

At our new church home, I felt an air of freedom. Coming up in the other church, I was so sheltered and bound by so many rules that, in retrospect, was nothing more than controlling tactics used by the former church's leadership. So many things were considered "secular" and/or "worldly"—as they liked to refer to it—that it's a sonder I was able to go about a typical day and interact with the rest of society. The other thing that bothered me so was the expectation that I was supposed to SHOVE Jesus down the throats of everyone I met. At the new church, it was "lead by example." This made me, as a teenager, feel more comfortable and open to exploring my spirituality and actually SHARING it with those that I encountered.

In the end, D and I didn't last long. He moved on and so did I, but I was still a part of the family and always around. Our families had grown close together. His cousin and I spend a lot of time together too. We grew close and began seeing each other. I know, I know...way to keep it in the family, right?! It really wasn't anything we planned. We just grew on each other. He and I just clicked. When I split with D, he had actually given his cousin the green light to shoot his shot with me. He was a few years older and way more mature than D. No doubt that's why we got along so well.

4

BAA, BAA, BLACK SHEEP

"Save the drama for your mama."
-African American Proverb

Over the next five or six years, things between me and Bebe were becoming increasingly tense. While I'm not exactly sure why she took issue with *me*, I do have my speculations—and heavily based on John and some of his personal demons. Along with all the confrontations Bebe often initiated, there were also the awkward, semi-perverse glances and uncomfortable hugs from John that I had to navigate. I never made mention of anything "uncomfortable" that he did because she would never believe me. She never believed anything I said on a regular day and had a habit of accusing me of things that I didn't do—so why even bother with trying to tell her that her husband had the tendency to come across as a creep? I didn't bother. I just made it a point to never be in the same room alone with him whenever possible.

    My tension towards her was fueled by her constantly pitting me against my siblings—which now included another youngest sister, the baby of the bunch. These games Bebe played, without question, was the reason for the lack of relationship we had growing up and even now. To them, I was always described as the outcast of the family. The rebellious one. The disrespectful one. The one who was jealous of them. I'm still trying to figure out how she came to these conclusions. Better yet, how a mother could be so cold towards one of her own. Her mind amazes me sometimes.

One thing I will give her though…I was low-key jealous of my siblings—but not in the sense that she thought. I wished that I was able to have a relationship with my parents like they did. *They* were celebrated. *They* were supported. *They* were shown love and affection. I hid my resentment by keeping to myself or spending time with friends as much as I could. With my friends and their families was where I was accepted, appreciated, and allowed to be myself. The older I got, the more withdrawn I would become. Not out of rebellion, but in an effort to preserve my peace and to avoid her frequent confrontations. Little did I know, this would end up being the case throughout my adult years…even to this day.

By the time I got to high school, I had landed my first job working as a cashier and as a server at a local Golden Corral. I was only 14yrs old…well, 14 and a half. Working over the summer became another tool in my toolbox of escape. When I wasn't working, I was on the track. During my freshman year, I found out that I had an untapped talent—running. It became my favorite past time, and I was good at it! Don't ask Bebe or John about my performance on the track or how proud they were of me. They wouldn't be able to answer because they never came to any of my track meets. Seriously, none of them. I would run in a track meet and either catch the activity bus home or hitch a ride from one of my classmates. Sometimes they'd be there to pick me up afterwards, but that was rare. Now, before you go any further, know that their lack of presence wasn't because they were busy, working, or other valid reason. It just wasn't something they felt like doing. They didn't show up when I advanced to regional competitions—and they even declined permission for me to travel with the rest of the team to the state competition when my relay time qualified to compete. Track became a passion of mine, but it was a passion that I didn't have anyone else to help foster and encourage. Talk about stifling potential!

After a while, my resentment grew into something that I couldn't hide as well as I was able to in the past. One day, I must have had the worst attitude, ugliest face, or something...to be honest, I really don't remember what the trigger was. I remember one day, Bebe, John, and myself were all in the hallway. She was fussing at me about something I did, while he looked on behind her, standing in the doorway. I had to be about 16yrs old at this time. All I remember was her fussing and yelling. Fussing and yelling. This was her normal behavior, so I'm sure I was just tuning things out until she decided to end her tirade and I could go back to my room. I did my best to keep a straight face and hold in the irritation and anger that I was feeling in that moment. The next thing I remember, she was looking at me with this look of aggression and disgust. She began to advance towards where I was standing.

What?! Oh, so you wanna fight me like some bitch on the street?! Huh? Huh?!"—this she says, as she is shoving me repeatedly.

I retaliated. I couldn't help it. I literally felt defenseless with her advancing on me in the offensive and her cohort looking on like he was waiting to get tagged in. After a small scuffle, John pulled us apart. My mother and I got into a fight. Did you read that?

I. Had to fight. My mother.

She had often threatened to send me away to live with my dad. After our encounter in the hallway, I almost wished she would have followed through on her threats. I know my dad's place was a million times better than where I was, but I didn't want to leave everything that I had worked so hard to establish in school, work, and with my friends. I was determined to not allow her to tear apart our family or rip my happiness away, again.

5

2002

"When we are no longer able to change a situation - we are challenged to change ourselves."
-Viktor E. Frankl

2002...well that was quite the year. At the beginning of the year, I was already 18 years old and had been working in retail at a local JC Penney. Although I was 18, and by society's standards an adult, I didn't feel like an adult at all. I was still living at home with my parents—who couldn't care less about by age. In fact, it was almost as if the reins were being pulled even tighter by them since entering official adulthood. Day by day and with each month that passed, I grew more and more disgusted with my sheltered life. I had no freedom whatsoever. Not even the least bit. It wasn't like I could go out and hang out with my friends and do things that most do when they reach that age. These people had a very generous midnight curfew that they enforced. By the summer of 2002, I had taken all that I could take. I decided that it was time to take action and change my situation.

I went on the hunt for a new job. I knew that there was nothing that I could do with an hourly retail paycheck, without working like a dog and quite possibly having to juggle more than one job. I remember one day going to drop my parents' car insurance payment off at the local GEICO office, not far from where I lived. That's when it hit me...drop off an application too! And that's exactly what I did. I didn't have experience working in a formal office building, but hey, it was worth a shot.

As luck would have it, I was sitting in the orientation room with about ten or eleven other new hires just a few weeks later. Scanning the room, I would quickly learn that I was the youngest and probably least experienced in the room. I didn't care though, because at that moment, I felt just a little more like an adult for the first time in the year that I had officially been one. About a week into my new job with excellent benefits, I turned 19, I also got a taste of my first corporate paycheck. This was more money than I'd ever made. I don't think I'd ever done math and worked up a budget so quickly in my life! That day on the way home from work, I stopped and grabbed an apartment guide. It was time for me to go and be on my own.

I remember flipping through this book and marking all of the places that I could afford based on my newfound riches. I found the perfect spot—not far from the military housing that we lived in at the time, and only about a five-to-seven-minute commute from my job. My decision was made. I snatched the deposit and first month's rent out of the bank and took it to the leasing office on my lunch break, signed my lease, and went back to work as a woman with my own place. October 19th was my day of emancipation. Now came the daunting task of having to tell my parents and deciding just when that would happen. Believe it or not, but the thought of me having to tell my parents that their grown daughter who was gainfully employed and could more than provide for herself, had found her own place to call home and begin living a life of independence...that shook me to my core! I knew that meant that I would be met with resistance. That's just how controlling of an environment we're talking about here.

The time came one evening in the beginning of October—when I would be forced to make a move and reveal my grand plans. We were all at home and my siblings and I were called downstairs. My parents had big news: they bought a house, and we were moving at the end of the month. Surprise! Surprise! Looks like my folks had their own secret moves that they were making. So long Virginia Beach...hello Portsmouth! My brother and sisters were all excited as my parents went over the layout of the new home and where each of our own rooms would be. Yes, you read that right...*our* rooms. By the time they got to my room, I had my own update. You guessed it...this was going to be the moment I decided to drop the bomb. The moment I officially entered adulthood. It wasn't dramatic. I simply said to them that I unfortunately would not be moving into the new home because I already had a place of my own to begin calling home at the end of the month. They were caught off guard and they...were...PISSED! There was the *"how dare you not say something?!"* response, which was swiftly followed up by the resistance that I had already anticipated. Doubt flowed with regards to how I would be able to support myself—never mind the fact that I had a well-paying job. Then they threw a curveball. The real reason for their resistance and lack of enthusiasm and pride for their oldest daughter finally establishing herself as an adult in this thing called life finally surfaced.

As it turns out, when making their decision to purchase this home, they took into consideration *my* newly increased income when determining whether or not they could afford to buy it. I can't say I was surprised by that move. I really didn't care anymore. I was actually quite disgusted at the fact that they would spend my money without even consulting me! Selfish! That's what it was! And it was in that moment that I didn't feel anything other than happiness for myself, for my grown-up decisions, and especially for the decision to secretly acquire my own place. Only God knows how things would have gone had I chose to involve them in the decision to move. Just like that, the tables were turned and the mood in the room was changed. They were deflated. I walked away...GROWN.

October 19th had finally arrived. I settled into my new digs quite nicely. It was a cozy little one bedroom one bathroom apartment near one of the area naval bases. I remember spending an evening clipping coupons and then using an entire paycheck to go grocery and bulk shopping for my place. I was so sheltered that such small tasks made me feel so accomplished. The first few nights in my place were spent putting things in place. Nothing was fancy by a long shot—I decided to thrift the big stuff just so that I'd have something in place, then go shopping for new furniture after a month or two. After all, it was just me and I was not looking to impress anybody...I was just happy being out there on my own. When I wasn't making my humble abode cozier, I was busy working. I lucked up on a new shift being offered at my job that offered a four-day work week and extra pay, with Thursdays, Fridays, and Saturdays off. These days would quickly become my party days—after about a week or so of getting used to the 12-hour workdays. Soon, my place became the place to chill. Pre-gaming at my spot before heading out was a must, as was the post-club wind down. This humble little apartment would soon be host to many impromptu gatherings, complete with copious amounts of alcohol. That's right, alcohol. If you've been keeping up, you'd know that I was still a couple of years away from the legal drinking age.

6

2003

"You cannot judge people because they sin differently than you."
-Erykah Badu

There's this belief that the more sheltered someone is growing up, the more they will let loose and "wild out" when they are out on their own. Well, this was proving to be true in my case. I was almost always trashed on the weekends and "functioning" on weekdays. Since I was underage, I had to rely on others to buy alcohol for get togethers at the house. But when we were out, this was never an issue. My weekend routine went a little something like this…

Thursdays kicked off my clubbing schedule with a trip to one of the local spots down at the oceanfront. Shaquey—one of my best friends, still to this day— and I would pre-game at the house and then head out. This was the one club that was strict with verifying age. I'm talking about drawing a giant black X on the back of each hand with super strong paint permanent marker, that way the bartenders knew not to give you any drinks. This place had a little black dress contest that they hosted every Thursday night as a part of their Ladies Night promotion…and every Thursday night, I was a part of the show. The winners were decided by the crowd and the "panel of judges" that the host would choose to pick the winner. The runner-up and second runner-up would each win $100, and the winner would pocket $250. If you were lucky enough to bag the whole $250, then you couldn't come back and re-compete until the end of the month with the rest of the weekly winners for a chance at $500. Me, I would always shoot for second or third place, if not tie for first place, that way I could continue to come back every week to re-compete. I legit would pay my rent every month with my winnings...ahh, good times! Now Fridays and Saturdays... they were out of control. Seriously.

Lagoons was the hood spot that the entire crew would frequent. I don't know how or when it happened, but I became super cool with all the bouncers that worked there. I never knew the reason (to this day, Shaquey insists it was because one of them was sweet on me), but whatever it was, all I had to do was make a phone call before leaving and whoever was on the door knew to have our wristbands ready. Standing in lines? NEVER! Me and my crew always walked by the lines of people waiting in either the freezing cold or summer heat to get inside, straight to the bouncers at the doors to get our wristbands and head inside to party. Yep, wristbands—which were *supposed* to be reserved for the 21 and up crowd. Why? Duh, alcohol. My first stop of the night was always to the bar. The bartender that worked there had a little crust on me, so naturally I drank for free. When he wasn't on duty, then my drinks went on the bouncers tab. I had a routine: two Coronas, followed by five cranberry and vodkas, and then two or three apple martinis. This was all consumed early in the night and fast! Me and my girls were notorious for setting it off in Lagoons...on the floor. We had a ball all the time. Well, from what I was told and from what little bit I can remember—all because I was always wasted. Once, Shaquey said that she had to help me walk out of the club and to the car so that she could get me home. When she was able to get me in the door, she said that things got really ignorant. The next day, Shaquey came over to give an account of what took place the night before. Now, you must keep in mind, this was around the time that cell phones were just being developed with the ability to voice record, so she had evidence...undeniable evidence to back the nutty story she was about to recall. Thank GOD there weren't camera phones yet! I was told (and I heard) that once she got me in the house and in the room, she was trying to help me into my pajamas and out of my sweaty club clothes. At one point, Shaquey asked if I could see her okay. My response to her was in song:

"Yeah, I can see you...I can see clearly now the rain is gone..."

Then I abruptly jumped up and said I had to pee. On the way to the bathroom down the hall, you can loudly hear me run smack into the wall. Of course, I have absolutely no recollection of any of this, and in all honesty, would not have believed one word of this story had it not been for the recording that captured all of it. I'm sure there were other funny moments, but there's no way for me to remember them because I was always grossly under the influence. It got to the point that cranberry & vodka cocktails woke me up in the morning and put me to sleep at night. It wasn't something I was or am proud of. Choice made during these times were most definitely regrettable. I can't tell you how many times I would drive home drunk. Times I would drink my pain, loneliness, and unhappiness away. No doubt about it...drinking just made the situations worse and took my drinking to higher heights—making it harder to shake in the end. I eventually would, but not without falling off the wagon a few times later. By early 2003, a lot had changed about me. I was now a low-key party animal with a drinking problem and had done something that I didn't think I would ever have the gumption to do...I lost my virginity.

Yep, it's true. Amid all this wild behavior, I had held out for as long as I could. I had been seeing this guy for a few months. Super cute, Dominican (which was, is, and will always be my weakness!), and overall, the sweetest, most respectful and understanding man I've ever crossed paths with to date. I remember when I finally decided it was go time, he was so concerned with my decision to finally go for it. Up until then, there were times where we would spend the night together and the sexual tension was most definitely there...so thick you could cut it with a knife! But even still, he respected my desire to wait on having sex. Never any guilt. Never any pressure. It was one of the million reasons that my feelings for him are so big.

When I was finally ready...to say it was amazing would be an understatement. We've all heard both great and horror stories about our first times—I'm talking about the ladies here. The lingering thoughts about all the negative, painful, traumatizing, etc. experiences that I had heard of from others was no doubt in the back of my mind. But this...this wasn't any of that. He was already so suave, even keeled, and affectionate on a regular day. When it came to our most intimate moment...let's just say I have absolutely no complaints or regrets. Not to sound cheesy, but it was truly the best first experience. All of the other times we were together weren't bad at all either, but that's for another time. The only thing that sucked was the fact that he was military and ended up having to ship out for a deployment not long after things really got going. Six long months. Now, we were never officially "official," which is weird because we were together a ton, and when we weren't together, we were always in communication. Nevertheless, the conversation about exclusivity and an actual relationship status was never had. So, with that, after a couple of months of more partying and socializing, I came to yet another turning point in my life.

By about late April of 2003, I kept having this gut feeling that something just wasn't right with me. I mean, I didn't feel sick or otherwise out of the ordinary. It was just this nagging feeling—rather, thought in the back of my mind that something was off with me. Over the course of about two or three weeks, I thought that maybe I was pregnant. It was an off the wall hypothesis—be it that my monthly cycle was always on schedule, I wasn't sick, didn't have any cravings or any other symptoms of pregnancy—but I was trying to think of everything as a starting point to figure out why I felt this weird feeling. I took five pregnancy tests over the course of this 2–3-week timespan...all of which were negative. I thought that maybe I was just being paranoid...and with that, I left the matter alone. Another week goes by, and I came down with one of the worst colds ever! This thing knocked me off my feet. I was downing cough medicine and cough drops like my mind was bad. Eat, medicine, sleep, wake up, eat, medicine, sleep. That was my life over these couple of days. On one day in particular, my girls had gone to a Cash Money concert while I stayed home solo to nurse myself back to health using my cough-medicine-sleep-repeat treatment cycle. I remember at one point I had to get up and go to the bathroom. With all of the medication I had flowing through my body, I was super lightheaded when I stood up. I made my way to the bathroom and sat down to pee. As I was going, I decided to go ahead and pee on the last pregnancy test I had for good measure. I thought to myself *"it'll be negative anyway."* I sat the stick down on the side of the bathtub while I cleaned myself up. I washed my hands and got ready to walk out of the bathroom to go back and lay down on the couch when I remembered that I hadn't thrown the test away. I turned around and picked up the test and went to toss it in the trashcan when I noticed...there were two lines. THERE WERE TWO LINES!!! I was in shock. I immediately grabbed my calendar and started counting days. There's no way this thing was right. My period had been coming like clockwork and I had just taken five other tests that were all negative. I counted and calculated frantically and to my surprise, my period was due that day and it was nowhere to be found. In my medicine induced stupor, I had completely forgotten what day it was. I looked at the test again and the test lines were getting darker and darker by the minute. No denying it...I was pregnant. I called Shaquey, who was just wrapping up her concert shenanigans. She answers:

"Hey, what's up?" she asked.

"I got two lines." I said, with a sense of disbelief in my voice.

"What??" Shaquey asked again, even more confused.

"I got two lines. I got two lines!"

That was all I could say. I was literally in a state of shock. She asked me what the heck I was talking about, and I finally got myself together enough to tell her what had just transpired. Shock was the predominant feeling and emotion all the way up until my first appointment with the doctor two weeks later. I went to the appointment alone. I had to be able to process all of what was going on. After paperwork and waiting what seemed like forever for the nurse practitioner to enter the room, nothing could have prepared me for what would come next out of her mouth. She proceeded to administer my exam, silently—then decided that an ultrasound was needed. I'm nervous at this point. "Well, it looks like you're measuring about 11 weeks, Ms. Moon." There was no more room for shock anymore. Complete and utter disbelief had taken over. It appeared my instincts were correct after all. My due date was Christmas Day, but on December 9, 2003—after almost 86 hours of labor, Leila Noel-Amaris made me a mother. This little person single-handedly changed the trajectory of my life, forever.

7

GUARD YOUR GRILL, GIRL!

"Sometimes I wonder if love is worth fighting for.
Then I look at you.
I'm ready for war."
--Unknown

    In 2005, when I was 21yrs old, I was living back in my parents' house with my now 1yr old daughter. I still had my decent paying job and was attempting to save up to move back out on my own. Correction: that is, saving what I could after having to give Bebe nearly half of my paycheck because I was living at home—along with other expenses like daycare, gas, and all. The family home was a large Victorian-style house in Olde Town Portsmouth, Virginia. When you walked in the door, you were in the formal living room. Nothing super fancy here...just standard living room staging. You walk through that room and enter the formal dining room— complete with a long table and giant china cabinet, and through the formal dining area to get to the family great room.
    Hanging with one of my best friends, Stacy, was one of my escapes from all of the drama and stress during this time back at the family home. We had been friends for a couple of years but grew closer after the passing of her mother. I love Stacy to pieces. We are a lot alike and a lot different at the same time. Really yin and yang—with her being

the softer side with a huge heart. One night while Stacy was visiting, the proverbial shit hit the fan between me and Bebe, and in a large explosive way.

As is the case with most of our blow ups, I can never really pinpoint exactly what straw was drawn to trigger a fight with Bebe, and this day was no different. I remember on this day in particular; Stacy had come over just to visit and chill out with us for a bit. She and I were sitting around talking about random stuff in the family room, and I remember my daughter started choking on her bottle and spit up a little on the floor. After making sure she was okay, I immediately began cleaning up the mess that was made. Stacy was seated across from the couch that I was on the floor near, trying to clean up. Halfway through cleaning, in walks Bebe. Welcome to the octagon!

Now, I'm going to be 100% transparent here...whatever the word exchange was that happened when Bebe walked into the room while I was trying to clean up the mess on the floor—I honestly cannot recall verbatim, or even partially. That's because it wasn't anything significant —or maybe I had just tuned her out like I usually did when she began ranting unreasonably. I do recall her yelling and fussing about the mess made. I remember calmly saying to her that I was trying to clean it up right then. Whatever was up her butt that day, I apparently agitated it by telling her that I was already trying to handle what she was upset about. Right then and there, amongst all her ranting and raving, I knew this—like all other verbal exchanges—would go left and end up with me shutting down, upset, and her declaring my not wanting to engage in her unreasonable raving and attempt to defend myself as "disrespect." I finished cleaning up and looked up at Stacy.

"Let's just go." I said as I picked up my daughter and began walking towards the doorway to the formal dining room.

This is about where Stacy was sitting. I looked over and told her to get her things and let's just go. I said this because Bebe was incessantly yelling and raging. About what? I couldn't even tell you. I had tuned it out at this point because it was seriously out of control, and I just wanted to get away from her and get my baby somewhere quiet and safe.

I could see Stacy beginning to get a bit upset—like she was about to start crying—because of the way Bebe was acting and what she was saying. With my daughter in my arms and Stacy walking behind me, we began to head towards the dining room, and towards the front door. At this point, Bebe cuts around Stacy and says something to me. I can't remember what it was…but I know I said to her that I didn't feel like going into a whole bunch of drama and that I would just go for a while.

Just as you walk through the doorway from the family room back into the dining room, there was this giant wood and glass china cabinet against the wall to the right. I had my daughter in my arms on my left side. The next thing I know, I am pushed into the china cabinet. And I mean HARD…WITH my daughter—her granddaughter—in my arms.

Today, Bebe wanted to fight.

I knew that there was no way this would end on any terms other than physical. I mean come on, if you get shoved into a glass china cabinet while holding your baby, what else is there to do? Luckily, just as I was pushed and right before hitting the glass, I was able to shield my baby girl from hitting the cabinet as well. The next ten seconds, I feel, would seal the fate of our relationship forever.

Stacy stood in the doorway in shock. Eyes as big as quarters. I will never forget that. In both anger and disbelief, I firmly said:

"Stacy, come get the baby."

That was all I could say. Those truly were the only words I could utter. Stacy reluctantly walked towards me, trying to talk me down—

while I repeated the demand, and Bebe continued hyping herself up to fight.

"STACY, COME. GET. THE. BABY!"

Still firm, not yelling, but definitely louder than the first time. Stacy —now crying along with my poor daughter in the midst of all of Bebe's yelling and chaos—stepped over and took my baby girl from my arms. I just wanted to get my kid away, somewhere safe, and in the arms of someone not emitting fury and anger. Almost immediately after Stacy took the baby, there came another shove from Bebe...

"Oh, you look like you wanna fight me like a bitch in the street!"

Here we go again! I will never forget that moment. I've lived it before, but this time it was different. She had absolutely no regard, no care, concern, or respect for the safety of my child. At all. I was furious. She wanted a fight and, on this day, I kindly obliged. Not because she picked at me. Not because she made me angry or pushed my buttons with all of her heckling...but because she had complete disregard for the safety of my kid. If you ever want to experience a ruthless and vicious version of me, mess with my kids. Claws will come out and damage will be done relentlessly and with absolutely no remorse. I don't care what you do or say to me, but my defenseless children? That's a no-go. That's crossing the line. That's poking the bear one time too many.

I. Went. In.

There we were...rumbling, swinging, hitting, slapping, and any other combative verbs you can think of. By the time I finally broke away, I realized I had called her every name in the book and told her exactly how I felt. We're talking about a good six plus years of pinned up tension, released.

I told her she wasn't shit.

I told her the only reason that she was upset with me was because I wouldn't let her have the control over me that she didn't have over my younger siblings--who at the time were quite out of control.

I challenged her parenting skills.

I called out all of her faults.

I said everything I could think of to get under her skin. I was pissed! I didn't care about me; it was the fact that she would do the crap she did and endanger an innocent baby. She was out of control and mentally unstable...no denying it. Instability aside, I needed this encounter to burn. I needed her to understand that she could not take me down.

I got my things, packed up mine and my daughters' clothes in a giant laundry sack as fast as I could, and started loading up my car. Meanwhile, Bebe has now moved on to throwing our things out the front door before I could get back inside to grab the rest of it. Baby stuff included. No regard. It was reminiscent of a breakup scene from a movie. February 2005 will forever be etched in my memory.

I left home that night with my one-year-old daughter in her car seat and all our belongings jammed in the car around us. We looked like hoarders. Stacy demanded I come and stay with her for a bit until I was able to figure out my next moves, and I am forever grateful for her hospitality. From there, me and my baby couch and bed surfed for a while—landing at both my girlfriend Shaquey and my girlfriend Monica's' homes for a spell. To this day, I am forever thankful for them and their families. We were homeless. I had a little bit of money saved, but nothing close to what I would need to stay in a hotel or even try to find an apartment to rent. My friends and their families—my families—they took us in. At that time, my friends were all the family I had. Thankfully, I was still able to keep working, but it was hard as ever trying to navigate the thoughts of where you're going to sleep, how to keep things stable for your baby, and work each day. This went on for a couple of months before I was summoned back "home" to apologize for the fight. Yes, me. I had to apologize for the fight that *I* started and for the things I said. Isn't that something?! I never received an apology from Bebe for frightening my daughter, nor did I receive an apology for her almost putting her through glass. Nope, she wasn't wrong for any of that...I was. That was our dynamic...I apologized for everything because everything that happened, and everyone's actions were always all my fault. Fine, so be it. I did what I had to do in order to have somewhere consistent for my child to wake up each day and go to bed each night. I put my child's wellbeing ahead of my own feelings and pride. Why? Because sometimes, we have to sacrifice our pride, feelings, emotions, wishes, etc. for the wellbeing of our children. That's what a mother understands, and that what a mother does, without hesitation.

When I moved back home though, things were very different. The room that myself and my baby girl originally shared—which was her nursery—was no longer available to me. My other siblings had their own rooms—with one moving into our former space. She didn't wait long at all to erase my existence. Me and my baby moved back to the family home, only to be crammed into a space that measured about as wide as a king-sized bed and just long enough to fit a twin bed with about two feet of space between it and the window—we shared that bed as sleeping arrangements. No exaggeration, folks. The room used to be a sitting space that was connected to John and Bebe's bedroom. This was what me and my baby were afforded when we were "welcomed" back home.

I dealt with this humiliation for only a few months, because during my time away, I was finally able to start saving up some money to get an apartment. This was no way for my child to live. So once again, I continued to save what money I could—after having to hand over half of a paycheck for "the house." As I did in the past, I began to make moves in silence. I couldn't afford to have her thwart my plans. Bebe's determination to make me completely reliant on her so that she could continue this cycle of abuse and humiliation was not going to continue anymore. I found a place that me and my baby could call our own. Not in a jail cell of a room...and not in the person that was that house.

January 2006, I packed my belongings up and began our departure. As expected, Bebe was less than thrilled about us moving. I could never figure out if it was because she wouldn't have someone there to control and humiliate, or if it was because of the extra money to pay for a home they couldn't afford wouldn't be flowing in anymore. This was a house that she wanted so badly but couldn't afford to maintain without *my* additional income. Sound a little presumptuous? Well, seeing as how they factored in my income when they originally purchased the house and then ended up foreclosing on the house soon after I moved out for good in 2009, I'd venture to say that was likely the case. Maybe it was a combination of both...the world may never know. Oh well, not my problem! We were out of there and that's all that mattered.

8

SECRETS AND LIES

"We must let go of the life we have planned...to accept the one that is waiting for us."
-Joseph Campbell

As if I didn't already end up in enough drama and crappy situations with my family, 2006 would bring me a blessing--but not before kicking off yet another series of unfortunate events that would continue to taunt me to this day.

Since early in the year, me and my baby girl had been in our new home for a few months. Things were great. We had a spacious two-bedroom apartment in Portsmouth, with a not-so-great view. The apartment was an upstairs duplex directly across the street from the family home. Ugh! But it was more than affordable and readily available, so it was home.

Things were great. Once again—and finally—I felt like an adult again. Like a mother. By this time, I'd been dating this guy...we'll call him J. We met while out partying at one of my regular club spots. He wasn't my type or typical go-to when it came to looks. Then again, I did meet him with a ton of alcohol in my system, so I guess there's that. He was a really nice guy. He loved kids and got along great with my daughter. He also met the parental units and actually hit it off well with them. That was a shocker.

This guy was smooth...he worked his way right on into our lives. We seemed to hit it off rather quickly, and sort of jumped into a relationship. He made himself present as much as possible. Then he took it up a notch and declared that he wanted to be a part of mine and my daughter's life—permanently. Yep, he proposed. It wasn't in any spectacular manner. No grand gesture, but in a conversation one day, he made this bold declaration. Now, he was *really* around a lot. Darn near moved in.

A couple of weeks goes by and a gut feeling that I knew all too well hit me like a ton of bricks...but this time it was accompanied by a level of fatigue that was borderline narcoleptic. I remember riding in the car one day with J and I just couldn't keep my eyes open. He said to me that I was sleeping so much because I was probably pregnant. Tuh, yeah right! I wasn't going down that road again...at least not yet. We were riding home from taking family pictures when he presented that hypothesis. When we got to the house, I ran straight to the bathroom and took a pregnancy test. NOT PREGNANT flashed across the digital screen of the test. Whew! False alarm and a bunch of I-told-you-so's.

About a week later, in early March, I was at work taking calls during the late night/overnight shift that I worked at the time. My boobs just started throbbing in pain. It hit me out of nowhere....and it hurt bad! They were so painful that I put my coat on at my desk to hide the fact that I had unhooked my bra because just the touch of the fabric was excruciating. My desk mate at the time jokingly said, "you're probably pregnant!" I shut that theory down with the quickness! It was around 3am when I finally got home from work. I headed straight for the bathroom, again. PREGNANT. Big, bold, and digital. I couldn't believe it. I picked up the phone and called my desk mate. She answered and I said *"damnit, I hate your guts!"* She didn't even say anything. She was cracking up laughing on the other end of the call because she knew exactly what I was talking about with just those words.

I had no idea how I was going to tell J. I didn't know how the conversation would go, but I was prepared for whatever was to come. I let him know the very next day when he came over after work as he usually did. To my surprise, he was elated. Two weeks later at my doctor's appointment, I would learn that I was only four weeks along. FOUR WEEKS. This was going to be the longest pregnancy ever! Little did I know, those words would be truer than I could have ever imagined.

My pregnancy with my son was completely different than my first. I was sick from almost the very the beginning and would be constantly sick through my sixth month. For those first few months, the only things I could stomach eating were french cut green beans, spring mix salad, and ramen noodles. On occasion I was able to tolerate meat and fish, but it wasn't very often. Nothing sweet, no juices, not even any cravings. Any of that would trigger debilitating nausea and the occasional migraine. All of this while trying to go to work when I could, plan a wedding, and still running into the frequent confrontations with Bebe. In April, J and I decided on an August wedding. We wanted to get married before my son was due to be born in November. Once we set a date, more and more friction began to build between the two of us. By June, I would reach my breaking point with him.

J disappeared for about a week from this family unit that he had developed. While cleaning up and going through paperwork that he had left at my house, I found something that would blow my mind. A marriage license. This fool was married!!! I couldn't believe it. And looking at the date, he had been married for a few years. I swear I can't make this stuff up! When I confronted him about it, he explained that he wasn't really "married" in the committed sense. He said that his godbrother had gotten locked up and he promised him that he would take care of his son and the baby's mother. So, while enlisted in the navy, he got married on paper to get the additional dependent pay and was sending some of the extra money to her (the wife) in New Jersey. I was livid. I kicked him out. The next day I took all of the things he'd left at my house, dumped it in a box, took off my engagement ring and set it on top of all of his junk. I sent him a text message and let him know that the trash gets picked up the next day and that he had until then to come and pick up his shit off the sidewalk.

Aside from being livid about my current situation, I began to go into a downward spiral. Sick, pissed, and depressed was how I spent the rest of my pregnancy. I knew now that he couldn't be trusted, so things had to be figured out so that myself and my children would be straight. To add insult to injury, I had dipped into my savings to begin paying for our "wedding" and with being so sick and missing so much work because of it, I barely had money to cover my living expenses. So, you guessed it...I had to move back home. Again. I had to finish the last two months of my pregnancy under the family roof. No, I wasn't happy about it at all.

After a couple of months free from constant nausea, the last few weeks of my pregnancy stormed in with a vengeance. I had a ton of--according to my doctors--unexplained swelling in my hands and feet that rendered me pretty much useless and unable to get around normally. This wasn't being remedied much because while I was at home on the modified bed rest that my doctor ordered, Bebe saw this as her opportunity to get some free labor out of me by asking me to sit at her computer for hours at a time and help her work on her graphics and website for a business that she started. Remember when I said no care or concern? Yeah, that part. Selfish! There was also a nagging little lump in my left breast that grew into something not so little as the weeks marched along.

Finally, after 39 weeks of pregnancy and four straight days of labor, I was able to meet my baby boy—but not before I almost bled out during the delivery. I just can't catch a break. But in the end, my little Micah Alexander was born happy and healthy. Looking at his little face made all of the hell and high-water worth it...although the hell and high-water was long from gone. His dad only came around consistently for about the first few weeks or so of Micah's life--this only because two weeks after delivery, I found myself back in the hospital. At the urging of both my doctor and my surgeon, I had immediate surgery to remove the pesky lump from my left breast, after an ultrasound determined that said lump was indeed a lump, and not just a clogged milk duct or other minor cyst. Being postpartum, angry, emotional, exhausted and then having to hear the words "biopsy" and "rule out cancer"...I ten out of ten don't recommend it. AT ALL! Thankfully, all tests came back benign. I tried to breathe a sigh of relief, but that wouldn't come for some time. All before my bouncing baby boy's first birthday, I would undergo three...count'em...THREE more surgeries, care of the lump that grew back two additional times and an attempt to ward off the potential for cervical cancer. Ladies, here is your friendly public service reminder to stay on top of your health and don't take any changes lightly. Talk about a rollercoaster ride of emotions to ride on your own!

Back at home things were what they were. This time, I actually had my own room with a bathroom located towards the back of the house. Logistically, this worked out great with having the little ones. I was grateful for this space because it was downstairs and away from everyone for the most part—even though I was paying a hefty rent for it. One amenity that I didn't pay for would have me question myself and make a decision that would forever change our family dynamic even more than it already had been—but it wouldn't happen for almost a decade later.

9

THE CROWN LIFE

"Uneasy lies the head that wears the crown"
-Shakespeare

Everyone always asks how I got into pageantry. The short answer: because of a blown knee.

In high school, I ran track as a sprinter, and I was pretty darn good at it. I had every intention of running track in college and had my heart set on working to snag an athletic scholarship. During my junior year of high school, I blew my right knee and was officially done with track…as well as with any dream of having a way to pay for college. My mother and stepfather sure as heck weren't going to help—they weren't great with money and barely had two nickels to rub together, let alone any type of savings for a child that they were preparing to send off to college.

With the track scholarship possibility out the window, I had to get creative with ways to fund my college aspirations. While walking down the school hallway one day during my senior year, I came across a flyer for an upcoming local pageant. The winner of this pageant would receive a $1,000 scholarship and go on to compete for more. Game on. But let us make note of the fact that I had never competed in a pageant a day in my life.

I did what I could and what I *thought* was going to work. For gown, I wore the dress that I bought from as store called DEB for my junior prom. That's one box checked. Next, there was the swimwear portion of competition. I shopped around and landed at this cute little swim boutique down at the oceanfront. There, I found this cute red one-piece that flattered me and that I felt confident in. Score! Finally, we come to the talent requirement. This is where I cringe. I decided to dance for my talent submission. Now, it should be noted that while I can dance, I've never had any type of formal dance training or dance camp under my belt. I enlisted a fellow classmate who was a cheerleader and on the high school team to help with putting together a minute and a half routine to perform on stage. I chose the song "Live Your Dreams"—you know, the song made famous by Julia Styles in Save the Last Dance. I don't know...maybe I was subconsciously channeling her character's determination and good fortune.

The big day was finally here, and I find out that this pageant is a preliminary competition to Miss Virginia...America! What have I gotten myself into?! I was not ready for the caliber of competition that I was up against. Have you ever seen the movie Little Miss Sunshine? To be honest, my pageant debut experience was eerily similar to the little girl in the movie. I stuck out like a sore thumb...but I had a BALL! I remember my family asking me how in the world I got on stage in front of all of those people and did what I did. Well, for one, you can't see a darn thing when you're on stage because of all the stage lighting that blinds you...so for me, it was a piece of cake. And just like that, I was bit by the bug...the pageant bug. There was now a pageant high that I needed to feel again, so the chase was on.

After much contemplation and review of my last performance, I declared that pageants with a talent competition category would be a no-go. It was time to find another competition that best suited me. This time, I did my research. About nine months later, I would go on to compete for the 2002 Virginia Teen All American title. This winner goes on to represent Virginia in the Teen All American pageant. This was it...this was the one. I upgraded EVERYTHING for this competition. My photos, wardrobe, interview skills...I wanted to go into this one seriously and prepared. Out of 52 contestants, I got runner up and an invite to compete at the national pageant in Miami, FL. My entire family was there to watch me compete and was surprised at my finish. Surprised, as in disbelief. It hit me at that moment—these people have absolutely zero confidence in me, and it showed in their snide remarks and reactions. It was then that I realized that I was alone in this journey...and that was just fine with me. I went on to Miami to compete at nationals with my mother in tow. While I didn't even place, I still had a ball. I also gained an increased drive and determination to see just how far I could go in this world called pageantry. Unfortunately, all of that drive and determination would have to take a bit of a hiatus while I lived out my wild and crazy times and have a couple of children.

In 2008, I stumbled across a pageant system that had a newly formed Ms. division in Virginia. This division specifically allows you to compete if you are 26 yrs. or older and single, divorced, or widowed, with or without children. At the time, a division like this was rare in pageantry. And so, it was...I came out of hiding and decided to compete for the title of Ms. Virginia United States. I won Miss Congeniality and got second place in evening gown. I didn't win the title, but the experience was all I needed to get the itch to compete again and chase that pageant high. I took a small break in 2009 and came back with a slight vengeance in 2010 when I competed for the title of Ms. Virginia American Coed. This was my very first time hearing of and competing in this system. Regardless, I did my research, hit the stage confident, and snagged first runner-up. I left that competition feeling like I was finally beginning to get back in my groove. A few months later in 2011, I circled back to the United States pageant. I stepped out of my comfort zone and decided to compete in a two-piece swimsuit. Come to think of it, I went into this pageant completely empowered. I went alone this time. I had only told a few people that I was even competing—and that was just so that they knew where I was while traveling for competition. No audience, no family or friend to cheer me on...just me and my confidence. I was in a different headspace this time, and one I had never been in before. I was up against some pretty heavy competition, but I didn't care. Third place overall. I was happy with it. The winner was a former NFL cheerleader, and her runner-up was a tall blonde beauty. Third place, for me, was acceptable in this instance and it still pushed me down a path for better. Little did I know, better would be closer than I could have imagined.

When the application window opened for the 2012 competition year, I felt like I was ready. I submitted my application and was thirsty for redemption. A couple of weeks after applying, I received a phone call that would be the steering mechanism for my future. The state director called me one afternoon. He remembered my performance in 2008 and the most recent 2011 competition. His phone call was to offer me the Virginia title for Ms. Virginia United States. I would go straight to the national stage. I literally squealed on the phone. This was my dream come true and a goal accomplished—to be a state titleholder on the national stage. I didn't know what to do with myself. I kicked, screamed, giggled, cried, and ran through my house in excitement when I hung up the phone. The way I was carrying on, you would have thought I just won the lottery. This offer was major for me. It was the opportunity to have access to a platform that would afford me opportunities that you don't typically get unless you have certain connections. As soon as everything was official, I sent out press releases to every organization and public figure I could think of...including the President of the United States, Barak Obama. And guess what...the President of the United States sent back a signed congratulatory note. When I saw the envelope in the mail, I lost it. The envelope was handwritten in ink. I carefully opened the envelope and read the card inside maybe twelve times. I even inspected the signature closely. Yep, it was most definitely signed by Obama himself. I couldn't believe it. I felt honored. With the message that he sent of encouragement to achieve every goal set; I knew this year was going to be something else! I was pumped.

I spent my first few weeks preparing for the upcoming state pageant—where I would officially be crowned the Virginia titleholder. In that time, Caryn, a co-worker and good friend of mine, fell ill due to a chronic medical condition. She would be moved to MCV Richmond—an advanced medical facility located at Virginia Commonwealth University in Richmond. Since my pageant was also in Richmond, I told Caryn that come hell or high water, I was coming to see her…and I made good on my word. After our first few days of mandatory pageant activities, I hopped in the car—still in competition wardrobe—and bolted to the hospital to see my girl.

I spent a little while sitting and chatting about everything you could think of with Caryn. I got her caught up with some of the shenanigans going on at work, reminisced on some good times, friend updates…just about everything. I remember she was so excited about my title. It made me smile and feel so great inside to have someone close to be genuinely proud of me and my accomplishments. When I got ready to leave, I have her a hug. It was such a big hug. It was an embrace unlike any other time we parted ways. As I was walking out the door, I looked back and said bye-bye again, but this time it was a bit ethereal.

I went back to the hotel to make curfew and finish up my weekend. On April 1, 2012, I was crowned Ms. Virginia United States. Even better, the person crowning me was Ms. Virginia United States 2011—turned Ms. United States 2011…the very same woman that I had competed against just the year before. So here I am, receiving my first state title and being crowned by the reigning national titleholder. This, to me, was epic because it's not something that happened often in pageantry. It also was sort of a foreshadowing of how great my year was going to be. I went home so happy. It was time to go to work.

Within two days of being crowned, I had already filled my calendar with appearances for the month of April and some of May. I did everything I could in the way of appearances. A couple of weeks into my title, I would get some news that shook me to my core. I received an early morning phone call from my girlfriend Sam. When I answered, I could tell she had been crying and trying to hide it. Sam called to tell me that Caryn—whom I had just visited, talked, and laughed with—was being given hours…maybe a day or two at best to live. She was on life support and her organs were all failing. It would be another day before I received another call…the call that tore my heart to pieces. Caryn had passed. I let out a wail that felt like it came up from the soles of my feet and through my body before exiting my mouth. I fell to the floor and just sobbed. I was in disbelief. We were just together sitting and laughing. She seemed fine…how could she be gone so fast?! All the unreasonable questions that I already knew answers to ran through my head, trying to make sense of what I was just told. I broke down again and sobbed…but this couldn't last long. I only had about an hour and a half before I had to be at a scheduled appearance. It was at that moment that I learned just how heavy the crown can be. I had to mourn and then quickly suck it up and get into hair and makeup so that I could make my scheduled arrival on time, ready to smile and chat with the public. One of the hardest days during my time in pageantry for me—but definitely not the last. Within my mourning, I heard Caryn clear as day. She lived by the rule of getting yourself together and dressing up when you're not feeling your best. And that's just what I did.

During my reign as Ms. Virginia United States 2012, I managed to make 72 appearances within 52 weeks…all while being a full-time mom and working full-time. I never told anyone, but there was a little something I did as a part of my reign to dedicate it to my late friend. When I went to visit Caryn in the hospital, I had on a pair of black rhinestone stilettos—she liked these heels a lot. I decided that I would wear these heels to every single appearance that I would make during my time as Ms. Virginia United States, taking Caryn with me, in a sense. I kept my word. They were worn to every appearance. Once my reign was over, I retired those heels and vowed to keep them as a memento with my crown and sash.

I was the first—and only to date—African American female to represent the state of Virginia as Ms. Virginia United States. My success as Ms. Virginia further afforded me the opportunity to represent the state of Mississippi in both 2013 and 2014 as Ms. Mississippi United States. So, for three years straight, I lived my life in the public eye and under a microscope. There were exciting days, long days, tiresome days, stressful days, and days that I just could take it anymore and wanted to quit. I quickly learned firsthand—albeit not on the exact level—why celebrities like Brittany and Lindsay snap and lash out. Having to be "on" at all times, having to watch every single thing you say, having to be extra cautious of everything you do—even still to have it misconstrued or misrepresented.... all of that is enough to drive a person mad.

Once my reign was up as Ms. Mississippi United States, I breathed the biggest sign of relief. I literally went into hiding for almost two years before finally deciding to get back out and reaffirm my name and identity with the public. At times, I get the feeling of pageant fever and have that urge to compete again…but then I immediately reminisce over the years after my retirement from competition and being a "has been." I have been able to pursue so many opportunities—including acting, becoming an entrepreneur, being able to serve as an executive team member for a major pageant system. In contrast, I also think about all of the personal battles that I had to endure on my own, behind closed doors—all while still having to wear a crown, sash, and a smile in public as a titleholder. When I think of all of that, I snap out of it, count my blessings, and continue to grow the projects that I currently have.

10

I...DO?

*"I'm not sorry for wanting what I deserve,
and I'm not afraid to walk away to find it."*
-r.h. Sin

By the time 2014 rolled around, I had been in a long-term relationship for four years, and that partnership began to take a left turn down a very, very difficult road. Just like any other relationship, we had our problems...but the problems weren't being acknowledged and resolved by *both* parties. I made a lot of changes and adjustments to myself and the people that I associate with to accommodate feelings and insecurities, but I didn't receive the same regard. Definitely not a an ideal situation to be in when trying to fix things and encourage change. Things were always up and down with us and it drove me nuts. This led to me beginning to shut down and check out of the relationship. In all of the hurt I have experienced in my life, I've learned that for me, shutting down and checking out is a defense mechanism that I use to shield myself from hurt and heartache. I shut down, was swimming deep in resentment, and teetering on the line acrimony.

Christmas 2015 came along and for the first time in all of the years that we had been together, he was home for our first Christmas together as a family. Things had seemed to be in a better spot than what we had been in the past year, so that was hopeful and a nice addition to the holiday season. This Christmas, our first Christmas together, he decided to propose. Now, before you get all excited and even more hopeful, this wasn't some spectacular proposal to share with the masses for years to come. It was quite the opposite. The kids opened their gifts early that morning and we moved right into breakfast--no different than any other Christmas morning. I had to take a moment to get on the computer to get some work done. While I was zoned into my assignment at hand, a gift box was placed on the desk between my arms as I typed. I opened it thinking it was a bracelet or earrings, as the box was a bit larger...but inside of the larger box was a smaller ring box, with an engagement ring inside. I slammed the box almost immediately. I was wearing my OnePiece jumpsuit with my head buried deep within the hood, so as not to be disturbed by things in my peripheral. Lucky for me, the hood gave some coverage to my face as well--which I caught dishing a not-so-pleasant reaction to opening the ring. I spun around in the chair and found him standing behind me, waiting for my reaction.

"I asked the kids if they wouldn't mind if I asked their mom to marry me..."

That was it. That was the proposal. Not a story that I gush and tell often.

After a couple of days of deliberation, we finally set a date...January 7, 2017 or 1/7/17. We *had* to have a wedding, but not because I wanted to He wanted a wedding and I simply wanted to go down to the courthouse and make it official. He wanted to go all out and have a big wedding...reception...party...the works, while I wanted to save all of that money and have a small get together with immediate family after we went to the justice of the peace. Here we go with another conflict...and I was the one that caved. Being the event planner and super organized person I am, I got to work on planning. I wanted to keep the menu simple, but thousands and thousands and thousands of dollars later, we had a humongous menu. We both come from huge families that live out of state, but would easily make their way to Virginia to celebrate the nuptials, so we had to control the numbers so things wouldn't get out of hand and expensive. I would have been happy with 50 people, but we ended up with a guest list of 150--which just so sneakily included his ex-girlfriend, who had been a significant friction point in our relationship over the years. Needless to say, planning this wedding was not something I was able to enjoy.

The one battle that I did win was the decision to keep our wedding party small. We landed on only having our siblings as our bridesmaids and groomsmen, and having my daughter as my Maid of Honor and my son as the Best Man. It was perfect...until thirty-seven days before the wedding. Both of my bridesmaids--my younger sisters--decided not to be my bridesmaids. One because she was big and pregnant and the other because she didn't like the dress that I chose for them to wear. I literally receive two text messages just a little over a month before the wedding that completely upended everything I had planned. I was devastated. I wanted nothing more than for my sisters to be there with me on my big day, and now that wasn't going to happen. To make matters worse, my mother decided to stir up some more drama by uninviting herself to the wedding, over a disagreement that we had regarding my sisters dropping out. But wait, there's more! She then proceeded to call my future mother-in-law, my aunt, and my dad to tell them that *I* told her that I didn't want her there. So, on top of trying to deal with my bridesmaids fallout and finding new ones, I also had to field phone calls from my family members about her and cockamamie story. I was determined not to let all of this get me down. I got in touch with two of my girlfriends who were able to purchase dresses at the last minute and they graciously stepped in to stand with me on our wedding day. As for Bebe, I ever so sternly advised her that while she was never uninvited, if she did choose to attend the wedding, it would be wise for her to call all of those that she previously spoke to, retract her statement and apologize. Of course she had no response to that suggestion.

As our wedding week approached, so did another crisis. Snow. The wedding was scheduled to take place on a Saturday. Early in the week, the forecast began to call for snow during the weekend. In Virginia Beach, that is the equivalent to the apocalypse taking place. At the same time, this area is notorious for getting just a dusting of snow and not a huge event. Well, on January 4th mother nature decided she wanted in on the wedding shenanigans as well.

I remember leaving the beauty supply store where I had picked up stuff for my hair on the Thursday before the wedding, and getting a phone call from my girlfriend-best-assistant-ever Sam. I answered...

"Hey Sam, what's going on?"

"What are you doing?" she asked me.

"Heading back home, why? What's up?"

"So, the museum called and since the weather is calling for a blizzard on Saturday, they are going to be closed that day. The want to know if you guys can move the wedding up to Friday."

There was a moment of silence on the phone as I listened to her deliver the news. I had just turned at the light and was headed down a pretty long stretch of road. I was in a daze.

"Khia?"

"Mmm hmmm, I heard you." I replied.

HIGH TEA

"Are you okay?" Sam asked.

"Mmm hmm. I'm gonna call you back when I get to the house."

I ended the call, tossed my phone into the passenger seat, and screamed crying for five miles back to my house. The city and the venue contacted us in the middle of the afternoon on a Thursday and wanted us to move our wedding up an entire day to Friday...that very next day. I couldn't take it anymore. All of these things kept happening and my mind started to wonder if this was even something that we should even be going through. Everything seemed like an omen. I finally made it home and within five minutes of me walking in the door, I hear the doorbell ring. It was Sam. She was at my doorstep with a giant bottle of wine in tow. She promised that we would get through this and make everything happen. Sam and I made every phone call possible to try and reschedule whatever vendors we could. Unfortunately, our caterer wouldn't be able to accommodate the earlier date because all of our food wasn't in. Sam came in clutch and found a restaurant that was willing to stay open and accommodate a large party. Unfortunately, most of his out of town family wouldn't be able to make it because they were all planning to drive in on Friday evening from New York and New Jersey.

So the day finally comes and things are hectic but moving along. As I was getting my makeup done, Sam walks into my dressing room. She ever so gently says *"Umm, Khia...Bebe is here."* I. Cringed. I hadn't talked to my mother or my sisters in weeks, since the whole ditching and drama fiascos, so I had no clue that the were coming. In walks Bebe like nothing ever happened. Talk about awkward.

When it was time to walk down the aisle, the plan was for my dad to be standing halfway down the aisle for me to meet him and he escort me the rest of the way down the aisle. That's what he rehearsed with the rest of the wedding party earlier that afternoon. Our entire wedding party has walked and taken their place at the front of the room, and now its my turn to walk down the aisle. To be honest, I was furious. I was upset about everything that had taken place and I was even more upset that things weren't exactly the way that we had spent so many months arguing about and planning.

As I begin to walk, I look over and see my dad standing there smiling and waiting for me. To my surprise, over to the left and directly across from him stands my stepdad, John, looking all late and wrong! He wasn't even in the same tuxedo as the rest of the wedding party. Everyone looked sleek and sophisticated in black-on-black-on-black tuxes, and there he stood in some navy blue suit. He took it upon himself to walk with me and my dad down the aisle. Fury may be the appropriate emotion here. He even took it upon himself to stand in front of my dad in the wedding pictures--something I didn't notice until after the fact. When I tell you these people ruin everything, they ruin EVERYTHING. They weren't the only ones to cut up during though. I learned later from a guest, two hostesses, and my bridesmaids that the invited "ex" was even being disruptive during the ceremony. My bridesmaids ended up telling me that they immediately went looking for her after the ceremony and told her to leave and not come to the restaurant afterwards. This explains why it took so long to find them for photos when it was time to get shots of the wedding party. In hindsight, I'm glad I had my girls there to step in and handle business when it needed to be handled. Those are the types of friends you want in your corner.

Not even one year into our marriage, we have a major blow up. I mean MAJOR. I tried to talk and work through the conflict at hand, but he wanted to argue and wasn't trying to hear anything. In the midst of our argument, he had the nerve to bring *her* (the ex) up and compare her to me. I was done and out the door. I had had enough. Once he realized this wasn't a bluff, then he was calm enough to want to talk--like I was trying to do to begin with. I made a vow to stick it out through good times and bad, yadda yadda yadda, so I stayed. But the damage was done, and I made it known. If I were a battery, I had about 50% charge left in me after that quarrel.

As the years have gone by, I admit we are still stuck in the same cycle we have been in. Don't get me wrong, he's a good guy...but we have problems that need fixing that aren't getting fixed. I often compare our situation to two boxers in a ring. I'm in the middle of the ring throwing windmills and he's still sitting on his stool in the corner, sipping water. These years that have passed have really forced me to take personal inventory and acknowledge what I have contributed to our issues. Shutting down and repressing my feelings and gripes has most definitely taken a toll on us. However, the biggest mistake that I think I've made is losing my identity. So many times I have made changes to who I am and how I do things, just to ease his insecurities or keep the peace. In doing that, I've completely lost myself. Among other things, it makes me feel stifled and unheard--which we all now know is something that has carried over from my formative years. It's quite difficult to get over something when you're constantly triggered by it. Even worse, it sucks when the person that should be your escape and your peace is a source of the trigger.

11

"P" IS FOR PEDOPHILE

"There are wounds that never show on the body that are deeper and more hurtful than anything that bleeds."
-Laurell K. Hamilton

Back in 2007, a few months after having my son, Bebe and John started having issues within their marriage. This went on for quite some time. There was always a lot of bickering and arguing between the two of them—even more than Bebe's normal confrontation count. It was during this time that I would earn some new scars that I hid for almost eleven years.

When I finally returned to work from maternity leave, I switched to an early morning shift that would require me to be up around 5am each morning so that I had time to get the kids ready, dropped off at daycare, and to work on time. I would be waking up around the same time that John would be getting set to head out the door for work. Now, if you know me, you know I sleep hard as a brick! I typically have four or five alarms set just so that I don't oversleep. John, calling himself trying to be helpful—would come into my room to wake me up. No big deal, right? Wrong! There were a number of times that I would awaken to hands touching and sometimes groping my butt, inner thighs, etc. You get the drift. There were times that I thought I was dreaming that someone was touching me, only to wake up startled and swinging because it was really happening. Something was clearly up and not right—but to what extent I wouldn't know for almost a decade later.

After so many instances that were too many to be coincidences or manufactured memories, I had to get ahead of the curve. I would wake up super early just so that I was already awake when he'd peep his head in my room. He now had no reason to go any further than that. But with a toddler and an infant, and sometimes running off of just fumes, it was beginning to take a toll on me physically. That was the last straw. I had to leave, and this time for good. Once again, I began the search for a place of our own and started scraping up extra money where I could. The stars aligned and soon, I was able to get my apartment back. Sweet freedom!

I never said anything to Bebe about John's handsy problems, simply because of our dynamic. There was no way she would believe me. Knowing her, she would try and accuse me of trying to cause division within the family like she did with any of our other petty spats. The best thing that I could think of to do was to just remove myself from the environment all together and not go back. That's just what I did. It would be a cold day in hell before you catch me living under that roof again.

In late 2010 just before Christmas and while his ship was on deployment, John surprised us all when he popped up home without any warning. We would soon find out that he got kicked off the ship because of misconduct. According to him, there was another sailor who he outranked (he was a chief at the time) that "cried rape" to save herself from punishment when they were caught in a compromising and consensual position. Since he outranked her, he was the one who got in trouble. The matter was investigated further, and he ended up being discharged from the Navy as "other than honorable." Since it was a Navy matter, we would never know firsthand what happened, what was alleged, or what was said...only what he told us. He went on an apology tour with the family. I wasn't as forgiving as my other family members. In my eyes, this likely wasn't the first time something like this happened...it was just the first time he got caught. People get comfortable and get sloppy, and oftentimes, that's when they get caught. I was unimpressed with his charade. Bebe, on the other hand, decided to be forgiving and stay with the creep.

It wouldn't be until 2017 that his wrongdoings would come to light —and I would learn of other allegations of molestation at the hands of John. It was detailed to me the incidents and subsequent denials and disbelief on the part of Bebe and John. That was the last straw. I couldn't sit back and be silent any longer. I thought it only right to help corroborate the other victim's account of what happened because what was loosely described to me was very similar to what I had experienced almost eleven years before. So, it would only be right to give this victim a voice...especially since she was my sister. This was the moment I learned that this man really was a monster. This was the moment that took me all the way back to my 10yr old self, and validated that gut feeling I'd been carrying around with me for all these years.

I thought what had happened to me was because I was grown and the closest thing he had to Bebe. As much as I hate to hear it to this day, we do look just a like. Their relationship was struggling and I thought he was coming for me as an outlet. As it turns out, this was a disgusting trend that unfortunately didn't just stop with myself or even my sister (who at the time was a minor). It also included friends of theirs who would come over to visit or spend the night. His victim list also included my daughter.

Sick to my stomach. Furious. Livid. Raging. None of these words are adequate enough to describe how I felt towards both Bebe and John. Him for the deed and her for the torture of disbelief. July 12, 2017. This would be the day I confronted and cursed all to be damned. This would also be the last time that I'd speak to either of them. He was unaware that I was told about not only the instances involving by younger sister, but also her friends, and what he had done to my daughter. I had already been to the police and filed criminal charges against him and a restraining order was in hand. The restraining order was more for his safety because had I come within 100ft of that man, I couldn't guarantee he'd walk away unscathed, let alone walk away.

I was driving home when we finally spoke. This phone call was being recorded, at the instruction of the police. I let him talk. He gave me some sob story about how he is going to therapy for his problem and that he was sorry for what he'd done, and blah blah blah. It was all a crock of shit to me. I specifically asked him had he done anything to anyone else besides me and my little sister. He insisted, "no." I told him that my concern was with the fact that this was going on, all the while my kids had been coming to visit and spent nights there—with me not knowing he had a thing for kids. He insisted that it was *only* me and my little sister. Lies! Lies upon lies upon lies! He had no clue that I had already been advised of the other victims...including my child. He decided to lie.

I ended the call.

I was shaking mad.

It's one thing to lie to me...but when you mess with my kids—that's a whole other set of problems that you don't ever want to have to deal with. The bear was out of the cage and she was thirsty for blood. I started recording again and I called him back. He answered.

"Hello," he said.

I kept my composure as best as I could, calmed my breathing a little, and approached very sternly and direct.

"When were you going to tell me about the incidents involving my daughter?"

[stuttering and stammering] *"W-what do you mean, kh—"*

I cut him off.

"No stuttering! And don't try to lie to me because I already know there was something that happened! What. Did you do. To my kid?!"

He let out a large sigh. I thought he was preparing for another of his sob stories, but instead he began to lightly detail one incident about touching her on her bottom when he was going to wake her up one morning. Sound familiar? When he finished talking, almost reflexively, I asked *"what else?"*

Never in a million years would I have expected him to keep talking and begin detailing yet *another* incident. I swear I almost ran into a median and wrecked my car. I couldn't believe it. Shock is an understatement. I didn't even get a chance to allow him to finish talking. I was sick to my stomach. I cursed him out. I screamed. I said all types of things. Everything was running through my head and it all came out of my mouth. It took all of heaven to keep me from driving past my house and straight to theirs to wreck shop. In that moment, The Hulk had nothing on me. I was seeing red and I wanted to draw blood. Then, he said something that made me even more furious than I already was…and I didn't think that was humanly possible. In all of his attempt to explain it all away, he mentioned that he *"had talked to mom about the situation and we decided it was best to just keep it between them for the sake of the family."* I couldn't believe what I was hearing.

I hung up on him and called her.

Recording, on.

She answers, *"hello."*

"When were you going to tell me about what happened to my daughter?"

"What are you talking about, Khia?" She said this with the most disgusting attitude and tone of arrogance.

"Don't play dumb with me! I know all about what John did to my kid! When was anybody going to tell me what the hell happened?!"

This woman goes on to justify why she kept everything a secret from me. It was all kept quiet "for the sake of the family." I couldn't believe it. But then again, I could. This is Bebe we're talking about here. Remember when I said poor decision-making skills and complete disregard for care and safety…yeah. Here, we have reached the pinnacle. As it turns out, I would learn that all these instances happened almost three years before I was notified. All the while, she was continuously bringing my children around him—knowing what he had done and what he had the tendency to do. Needless to say, the conversation between she and I was bad. Really bad. I let go and let have. That was all I could do because if I did anything else, I'd go to jail or lose my kids.

To completely cut Bebe and John off and our of our lives was the only feasible option. Not that it was an easy choice, though. Not only did John's actions grossly violate people and destroy our family dynamics in the way that it did, but both his and Bebe's actions would forever change our familial structure. Along with dealing with the news that I was just made aware of, I also had to prepare to explain to my children why they weren't going to be able to go to Gam and Pop Pop's anymore and why they weren't even going to be allowed to communicate with them. This woman has a knack for destroying happiness and tearing families apart. The whole situation just sucked! Luckily, I have some of the best, most resilient children in the world. Since the great cut-off of 2017, these kiddos have been just fine. I make it a point to check in with them often, just to check and see if there is any lingering resentment that is going unspoken. Nothing to date. Gosh, I'm proud of them for being strong, but I hate that they had to be so strong at such a young age. I hate that their grandmother would sacrifice their innocence for her own comfort.

You see, Bebe didn't want not to tell what John did because she knew I would turn him in in a heartbeat. If that happened, he would likely lose his security clearance and his well-paying job—that means her meal ticket would be no more—and she hasn't worked a real job since we lived in California, so she would be required to start all over again. She was thinking about herself. Selfish. She went so far as to tell my sisters (who were privy to the happenings) that if they ratted him out to me, that I would make sure *they* would get in trouble too, get kicked out of the military (they were enlisted at the time), and go to jail. Now, what sense does that make? Remember when I said she has a nasty habit of pitting me against them... I could only shake my head when I heard of this. Right away, I explained to my sisters that they did nothing wrong and that it wasn't their responsibility to tell me what happened because they weren't the ones responsible for my kids.

Unfortunately, this creep still roams free. Since my daughter was so young and unaware of what was happening to her, John the Pedophile is a free man. Despite his own recorded confession and detailing of his acts in his own words, since he cannot face his accuser, there will be no conviction. So, he is free and able to add more victims to his roster. Yay justice system!

Sadly, my siblings still associate with their parents. It's sickening, yet I understand why it would be so hard for them to cut ties with these monsters. They honestly don't know any better. Growing up, they never saw the things that I saw, and they don't know the many faces of Bebe like I know them. They were never mistreated or treated like I was--well, with the exception of what he did to one of my sisters. The only thing they ever witnessed was me having to apologize for things that she did or caused. So, I was always the proverbial bad guy—which fully supported her narrative of me. I'd venture to think they dismissed his actions as isolated and that he got the "help" he needed and is all great now, and that Khia is just overreacting and being her usual unreasonable self.

They still gather for holidays and other celebrations, and even take family pictures—but it's as if myself and my children don't even exist. You wouldn't know that she has another child and more grandchildren. I'm sure she has developed some story to explain away her dysfunctional familial situation...and quite frankly, the level of delusion is saddening. In my opinion, only twisted individuals can sleep at night comfortably knowing the things that they have done and the damage that they have caused to others.

No care.

No regard.

Aside from three people, none of our family knows that Bebe enabled John to do the things that he did. Of course, the two of them would never tell anyone of the abuse, violations, deceit, and treacherous things that have taken place over the past 25 years. That would completely ruin the righteous persona and wholesome family unit that she has perpetrated over all of this time. It finally hit me, and I realized that by staying silent and making up random excuses for the lack of communication between our families, I was perpetrating the same fraud. No more. I was trying to protect a group of people who are all grown, fully aware of the choices they make, and capable of navigating the consequences of the choices they make. It's time to change her narrative and do what I've always been taught to do...something she's proven she's incapable of doing...and that's walk in truth.

Until the release of this book, none of our extended family was aware of these happenings. The tea—well, *a good amount* of it—has been spilled.

12

LIFE

"Mortality applies to every aspect of life. The fear of death is the driving fear of life."
--Nick Tosches

After having Leila and Micah, and considering the many health issues I ran into in the year after having him, I made the decision to jump on the growing popularity of the IUD as a form of birth control. I mean, who doesn't love the idea of not having to deal with a monthly period for up to five years?! Little did I know, this decision would kick me in the rear for years to come. In the beginning, it was great. There were no side effects and no extra expenses to budget for monthly. But about four or so years into my IUD journey, things began to change. I remember visiting my gynecologist office multiple times over about a six month timeframe for complaints of pelvic pain, and just not feeling myself. I told my doctors that I felt like I should either be pregnant or going through menopause. There was cramping, I was moody and emotional, random bouts of nausea, hot flashes, crazy sleep patterns, my weight was going up and down, and my hair was falling out, among other things. I told them that I felt like something hormonal was going on. The doctor just suggested that I just take the IUD out and see if that made things better in a few months--and passed on doing a lab workup because of how young I was. I agreed to removing the IUD, but after that appointment, I went on a mission to find a new provider. I checked with some of my closest girlfriends and found a new practice to take my concerns to.

My first appointment left me beyond impressed. I walked into the new doctors office with my entire medical record in hand from the previous doctor. The new doctor sat me down in his office and actually listened. I explained my history and just like before, told this doctor that I felt like I should either be pregnant or going through menopause with the way that I was feeling. Before I could say another word, the doctor suggested we start by getting some labs done. Sweet! He also took the large stack of office notes that I brought with me from the previous doctor and promised to look over everything. When I returned a few days later for a follow-up appointment, I was shocked. The doctor confirmed what I thought was going on...something was up with my hormones. One number that was supposed to be high was low and another that was supposed to be low, was high. He said the next step was to get an ultrasound of my ovaries to see if it was something that he suspected. Low and behold, he was right. I had PCOS (polycystic ovary syndrome). He showed me the ultrasound images of my ovaries. One had a few noticeable cysts on it and the other literally looked like a raspberry. My ovaries were covered with cysts. I guess he could see the shock and heartbreak on my face, because he immediately went into reassurance mode and came up with a plan of action to help me try and reverse some of the damage. I felt hopeful for the first time in months, and just a few months later, things began to improve greatly.

With my improved status came a new conversation that me and my then boyfriend had. We decided it was time to try for one more kiddo. Leila and Micah were growing up quickly, I missed having a little one around, and he didn't have any children of his own. So, naturally a baby was in order. My doctor cautioned us that given a previous surgery I had to have on my cervix a little after Micah's birth, any new pregnancy would be considered high risk and there would need to be extra precautions in place--likely in the form of bedrest. We understood and we were ready to do whatever it took. We got right to it. Too bad my body didn't get the memo. After about a year of trying with not so much as a possible "scare," I landed right back at the doctor's office. This time, I wouldn't leave as content as I would have hoped. This time, I would be adding another specialist to my medical roster...one who specialized in infertility issues.

    Five years goes by and still our family is a family of four. There wasn't any progress being made on the baby front and I had began experiencing some unexplained pelvic pain. My doctors checked all that they could hormonally and visually via ultrasound, but nothing could be found to identify the source of the pain. So, in January 2018, I would go under the knife so that my medical team could lay eyes on my insides and see what the heck was up. Enter endometriosis. Fun...NOT! They got out what they could and while they were in there, fixed the source of my pain by separating the fusion of my ovary to my intestine due to the endometriosis. We were hopeful that with all of this, we could make some progress. To hedge our bets at a successful fertilization, we even took it a step further and in April of that same year, underwent fertility treatment and opted for an IUI. Too bad it was money down the drain. He was all ready to give it another shot and try for IVF, but I couldn't do it. All of the office visits, the hormones, the testing, and the heartbreak was already too much for me mentally. I couldn't handle the thought of placing actual embryos, hoping to become pregnant, and possibly miscarrying. That would break me. I took a look at my life and considered maybe I was only meant to have my two children, who I loved so dearly. So, with that our journey ended. I would spend the remainder of the year watching so many people around me announce their pregnancies and celebrate their gender reveals--each one twisting the knife in my gut over and over again. I longed to experience the ups and downs of pregnancy again and slipped into depression.

Our anniversary rolled around in 2019 and we decided to go to Vegas to get away for a few days. It was a welcomed distraction for me. When I returned home, it would be just me and the kids due to a scheduled deployment. I flew home to Virginia and he had to hop a flight to New Jersey to meet the ship. The time away made me feel a little bit better, but I still needed something to get my mind off of my woes. So, I took to Pinterest and decided to try my hand at some DIY projects. After a bit of deliberation, I decided to build a pallet bar for the house. I was amped. I had this newfound burst of creative energy and I went all in. Hauling pallets, trips to Home Depot, and playing with power tools was just what I needed. A few days into the project, I started to notice that things were feeling a bit off, again. I just felt inexplicably weird. The random bouts of nausea were back and so were the hot flashes and mood swings. In one of our daily emails back and forth, I remember telling him that I felt off again and was going to set a doctors appointment because I thought that maybe my hormones were going down hill like they did years before. I even took a pregnancy test knowing that it would be negative, just so that we didn't have to journey down that conversation when I got to the office. I was right about my hormones once again...but not in the sense that I thought. When I peed on this particular stick, it was hella positive. A big'ol bright plus sign was staring me in my face as I sat on the toilet in disbelief. I would sit still on the toilet for 15 minutes before I finally snapped out of shock and realized what was going on. I peed on another one. Positive. Was this really happening? Was I seriously pregnant?! There was no way...it had to be a fluke. We had been trying for almost seven years and even with fertility treatments, didn't get anywhere. Nope...this was just my hormones playing a cruel trick on me. I decided I wasn't going to get myself all riled up until my appointment. At the appointment, the first thing that was done was a repeat test--urine and blood. Turns out, it was true. According to the tests administered at the office, I was indeed pregnant. But I wasn't going to believe it until I saw it with my own eyes. Lucky for me, the doctor wanted to check and see exactly how far along I was because I had just had a period not one month prior. There was an opening in the ultrasound schedule and they were able to squeeze me in the same day. On February 11, 2019, I learned that I was an estimated six weeks and two days along. There I was, staring at my little miracle on the screen. What happened in Vegas, clearly didn't stay in Vegas!

    As excited as I wanted to be, I couldn't help but remember the doctor's cautionary words years ago when we first started in this journey of trying to have a baby. This was going to be a fragile time and I was going to proceed with every bit of caution I could muster up. I hadn't told the world just yet and I planned on keeping it that way for just a little while longer, but my body wouldn't cooperate with that plan. When I hit seven weeks, I sharted showing big time! I'm not talking about just a little food baby pudge...not just a cute little baby bump. I'm talking SHOWING showing. So, I was forced into hiding. I only entertained visits from the handful of people that I had shared the secret with--one of which was NOT my mother-in-law. Her birthday was at the end of February and we decided that we wanted to share the news with her as a gift. This made things extra awkward at times because she would often come by to visit. The only way I could hide by burgeoning belly when she came around was to wear my bathrobe. So here I am, looking super lazy every time she came around.

    March 3rd couldn't get here fast enough. This was the day that we took my mother-in-law out for her birthday dinner, and it was also the big reveal day. I had it all planned out perfectly. We took her to this seafood restaurant called Captain Georges. It's one of her favorite places to eat. There I was with the kids seated in one of their back dining areas that was sort of laid out like a banquet room. I had picked out the cutest card for her and left it at her space at the table, along with a bouquet of beautiful flowers. On the outside it said: *Where would we be without you , mom?* And on the inside: *One of us wouldn't* exist and the other would be married to some loser. Just under that on the inside of the card, I wrote: *Plus, you wouldn't have another grandchild coming in October!* After she and my father-in-law arrived, we all sat around talking for a bit and having drinks--of course I was only sipping water. A few minutes passed and I asker her if she was going to read her card. It took her a minute to get it, but after she found her reading glasses, put them on, and read what I wrote, she let out the biggest shriek I've ever heard. Everyone in the area where we were dining turned around to see what was going on. She jumped up from her seat and ran around the table to give me a hug. It was at that moment that she really realized this was happening. As I stood up and she saw my big nine week belly, looking like I was at least four or five months along. She continued to hoot and holler, yelling *"she's gonna have a baby, I'm gonna be a grandma again"* to the other restaurant patrons looking on. The entire dining area erupted in applause and cheers. It was such a pure and beautiful moment.

Now that all of the family knew, it was finally time for the world to know. I took to Facebook and posted an ultrasound picture with the following caption:

"Ok, guess it's my turn!

We found out on the last day of January that 2019 was gonna be one for the books. Finally able to tell the masses that Lil'Smitty will join us in October. By every standard, this little migro human is definitely a miracle baby. Dad is excited and I'm [a nervous wreck]--all at the same time and while at home on "reduced duty" (visitors now welcome since I'm no longer in hiding). VERY FEW knew...and for your ability to hold water until we could tell Marr's mom today for her bday, I thank you!

SN: still trying to wrap my brain around this already high maintenance little gummy bear and plot out the rest of what is a crazy busy year, so if I don't call/text/respond/go out/ whatever like I used to...I'm sick, exhausted, and on a roller coaster of emotions. Sue me. Love you, mean it!

#LilSmitty #3 #AnotherOne #LoveOnTop #October 2019"

It felt so good to finally be free to sport my big belly around loud and proud. This liberation would soon be interrupted by a tsunami of emotions that still hit me on occasion to this day.

Just four days after our grand announcement and surprise to my mother-in-law, my world would be rocked harder than I could ever imagine. Earlier in the day, I had to go and satisfy my almost daily craving of broccoli cheddar soup. I came right back home and shortly after, the kids got home from school. I was feeling quite tired, so I put on my comfy robe and laid down on the couch for a quick nap. At around 7pm, I was startled out of my sleep by a mild cramping feeling. My bladder felt full, so I thought I just needed to go pee. As I was getting up from the couch, it felt like I was peeing my pants. I rushed to the restroom as quickly as I could. I pulled my leggings down and sat down. Sweet relief. I looked down at my underwear and leggings and there was blood. A lot of blood. I looked in the toilet and even more blood was there. I wiped and more blood and small clots. Panic was an understatement. I immediately called my doctor on call and explained the situation. Straight to the emergency room was my only instruction. I jumped up and kicked off my underwear and pants and began to wipe myself up so that I could head out. Tears and almost uncontrollable crying was a flow. As I went to put on new underwear and pants, I felt sort of a pinch in my lower pelvis. A few moments later, I felt a large blob pass. Right there in my underwear, there was a large mass of bloody tissue, about the side of the palm of my hand. I don't think I could ever recreate the wail that I let out. I had never experienced a miscarriage before, and I thought I may have been looking at my little miracle. I almost passed out. Clearly, I was in no condition to drive. I called a girlfriend of mine who lived less than five minutes away.

I sat in the waiting room for what felt like an eternity. It was almost two hours before I would be called back to a room. There, I sat for almost another hour, waiting to see what the game plan would be. Someone came in and took a bunch of blood for labs. Then, finally, I was wheeled back to the ultrasound room. The first thing to do was clearly to check for any signs of life. While back in the ultrasound, the techs are instructed to not share any information, details, speculations, etc. with the patient. A doctor was the only person authorized to review all of the findings and provide their professional decision and next steps. It made for the most awkward ten minutes of silence ever. Even though I knew the protocols, I couldn't help but take a shot and ask if there was anything hopeful. Of course, the tech--with the screen facing only her and away from me--could only respond with *"I'm sorry, you have to wait for the doctor to review and go over everything with you."* I was devastated all over again. They wheeled me back to my room for more waiting. After about another 30 minutes or so, in walks the doctor with a nurse. They don't usually come in two's unless its bad news. My heart sank as soon as the door swung shut.

"172 beats per minute." he said.

Those were the first and only words out of his mouth as he looked on with a smile of relief. I burst into the biggest flow of tears imaginable. A subchorionic hemorrhage was the official diagnosis, and apparently I had passed a large hematoma. Apparently, this is only seen in an average of 18% of pregnant women. The ultrasound showed an additional smaller hemorrhage still, so the doctor ordered me to continue my bedrest and to immediately follow up with my doctor. My appointment came two days later and included another ultrasound to check on Lil'Smitty. This time, I was able to see my baby, and boy was I overwhelmed. My little ten week old jelly bean was in there wiggling around, and I could make out where the hands and feet were. Queue the waterworks again! As an extra layer of precaution, the doctors decided it was full bedrest from here on out.

I had another follow-up appointment a few weeks later to go over some of the extra lab testing they complete for those of an advanced maternal age. One of the built in perks to all of the testing is that you get to find out the gender much sooner than normal. So, I already knew going into my 16 week appointment that Lil'Smitty was a bouncing baby boy. And bouncing he was! That ultrasound was like none other. Even though I couldn't feel it yet, this kiddo was tumbling all over the place. It was so exciting to see. I was on such a high. Things were finally starting to look up. Then the doctor walked in and put a pin in all of my excitement. The ultrasound showed two fibroids and a new heavy hitter to worry about--placenta previa. Was I ever going to be able to catch a break, ever?! Nope! At least not any time soon.

    A little before my 21 week appointment, I started experiencing Braxton-Hicks contractions. When appointment time came around and I gave that update, the doc decided that if the contractions kept up or if any changes were noticed in my cervix, we would immediately move to weekly injections that would help to keep the contractions to a minimum, since I had a history of pre-term labor with both of the older kids. After that appointment, I headed home and took it down for a nap. I was getting bigger by the day and moving around was exhausting. I was awakened from my nap a few hours later by a contraction that was a little more intense than they had recently been. A few minutes goes by and here comes another. Then another. And another. Contractions were coming rhythmically now and every 11 minutes. After an hour of consistency, I called the doctor on call. Back to the emergency room I go. I lived only about seven minutes away from the nearest hospital, so I figured I could easily drive myself there between contractions since they weren't *that* bad. I'm glad my friends vetoed that idea because these suckers ramped up in intensity no sooner than I could get out the door and to the car. It was hard to concentrate on my fear of the fact that I was in pre-term labor because the pains were coming faster and harder...now about every seven minutes. I slow waddled to the labor and delivery floor after making two contraction stops, where they were ready and waiting for me. Thinking I was just being dramatic, the staff very nonchalantly hooked me up to the monitors. After about 20 minutes of monitoring, things started moving fast. Imaging was ordered, labs were drawn, and medicines were administered. We made it through the entire gauntlet of medications with no success. Labor pains were still coming and coming hard. The only remaining option would be to admit me and put me on a magnesium drip. The goals changed from just trying to get the contractions to stop, to trying to get me to 23 weeks so that my baby boy would have a fighting chance, if he were to end up coming early. ROCKED TO MY CORE. That's the best way to describe how I felt, but it's in no way accurate. I spent three days in the hospital all by my lonesome before things would finally calm down enough to where the doctors felt it was safe enough for me to go home. This time though, the bestrest conversation was a bit more stern than before. Point, taken. Those weekly injections followed shortly after my return home...and boy were they a doozy! Imagine taking an Epi-Pen jab to the back of the arm, you know, in the meaty part just off the armpit. It was the worst...but nowhere near worse than the thought of having to meet my baby sooner than he was due. So, human pin cushion it was!

By the second week of August, I made it to 32 weeks. That appointment was finally one where there wasn't any bad news to be shared. The placenta previa had corrected itself and although the contractions were still coming, they were far less intense and not anywhere near organized...so the injections were working. That visit's ultrasound of Lil'Smitty showed that he was already measuring over six pounds. Since he was so big and we had already implemented medications to help mature his lungs, the doctor decided that any labor after 36 weeks wasn't going to be stopped--especially since there was now a concern that at the rate he was growing, we might be in the nine pound range. This would throw off all of my plans for a natural, possibly at home birth. Crazy, I know...but since I had decided this would likely be the last baby, I wanted to go all out. I had the greatest doula and she and I worked together to create a solid birth plan. I was going to go drug-free for as long as I could tolerate. I absolutely did not want an epidural. I wanted to be able to fully experience the miracle of childbirth in all of its painful glory.

One part of the "painful glory" I didn't realize was a part of the package deal was a little something called SPD, or symphysis pubis dysfunction. Basically, my pelvic joints were moving unevenly. This made it ridiculously painful to walk, sit, lay, or anything else that involved my hips. Luckily, it was something that resolved itself soon after birth, according to all that I read about the condition. At the suggestion of my doula, I decided to try giving a chiropractor a shot at providing some relief. So, on the afternoon of September 19th, I lugged my big self on over to chiro. When I walked out of that office, it was better than I had walked that entire pregnancy. Albeit slight, I felt some much needed relief. It was enough relief to allow me to get out and go for a walk down the street--something I hadn't been able to do the whole pregnancy. I wasn't going to overdo it though. I just wanted to get out and enjoy the nice day that it was outside. During the walk, I had a pretty decent contraction hit--which let me know it was time to end the excursion and put it in park for a bit, and that's just what I did. I came inside and put my swollen feet up so that I could relax a bit. I noticed though, that my feet and ankles were swollen more than usual. Since my blood pressures had been within normal range, I just chalked it up to end of pregnancy changes and the fact that I had just been out on my walk. Later in the evening, I started to feel a little lightheaded out of nowhere. I grabbed a bite to eat, thinking that it was all due to hunger, but the lightheadedness only persisted. It then dawned on me to check my blood pressure. 152/92. I won't ever forget that number, because I knew exactly what it meant and what was going to follow. I called the doctor's office and just as I suspected they would, they instructed me to high tail it to the hospital labor and delivery floor. They wanted to rule out pre-eclampsia. So, back to the hospital we went--but this time I brought my bag with me just in case. It was the usual process: change into a gown, pee in a cup, give a little bit of blood, and let the doc dig around and check to see if you're dilated any. Much to my surprise, I was at 2cm. We knew we were going to be there for a while, so with my contractions picking up in intensity a little over the past two hours, it was suggested that I go and walk the halls for a bit while we awaited all of the labs to come back. After about an hour, I returned to the room and got back on the monitor. Contractions were still coming and they were seeming to be a bit organized, although they were still quite a bit spread out. Just after midnight on what was now the 20th, the midwife returned to the room with the nurse and dropped the bomb on me that I already had a feeling was coming. Here we go with the pre-eclampsia. She decided to check me once more as she was discussing all of the protocols for pre-eclampsia. She let out a *"hmmph"* as she checked my cervix. When she came up, she asked me if I just wanted to go ahead and stay and have the baby. WHAT?! I was definitely not expecting that to come out of her mouth. All of my walking opened me up another centimeter and since I was progressing, having contractions, and had the positive pre-eclampsia labs, she made the call that I could stay and they would break my water. I was hyped! Within one hour, I was moved into my own birthing suite, my mother-in-law had arrived, my doula was by my side, and my water was broken. I knew that it wouldn't be long before the contractions would become super hard and the real work would be on the horizon, so we all took some time to get a nap in.

By around 9am, my regular doctor had made her rounds to my room. She wasn't too pleased with the lack of progress I was making and put the option of pitocin on the table to try and intensify the contractions some and get my cervix to dilate faster. I just as swiftly shot her suggestion down. I knew with pitocin would come the need for an epidural--which I absolutely did not want. So we agreed that we would revisit things in a few hours. Noon came around and I had been working with my doula doing everything possible to get things moving in the direction of progress. I was only 4cm. In came the doctor again with the pitocin talk. Her argument was that with my lack of progress and my blood pressure still being elevated, things had the potential to take a turn for the worse at any point. I was immediately deflated. Having pitocin equals having an epidural, which equaled having to be pinned to the bed with the inability to move around...which was not at all what I wanted. But I didn't come this far to not come home with a baby. So I sadly agreed. The nurses came in and hung the pitocin and shortly after, the anesthesiologist followed to administer the epidural. There I was, now trapped to my bed with the hopes of no longer feeling these insanely intense contractions that had now kicked in. Too bad that wouldn't be in the cards though because as my luck would have it, the epidural on took on my left side.

    I labored on pitocin with a half an epidural for another nine hours before I would finally hear those magic words: *it's time to start pushing*. I started off trying to push in that reclining position that is the standard "epidural pose" the staff likes to gravitate towards--you know, with your knees back to your armpits and your chin to your chest. It wasn't doing anything for me, and I've always been an excellent pusher. So, I decided to take control of the situation and start calling some shots. I told them to sit me all the way up and break the bed down, so that I was in the throne position--basically like I was sitting on the toilet. Since I didn't lose all feeling, care of the failed epidural, I could feel if my pushes were productive. In this position, they most definitely were. Lil'Smitty started moving right on down...and then he stopped. I pushed with the next contraction and still no movement. When the midwife went in to check and see what was going on, she felt that his head was just a little off center--causing him not to come through my pelvis and into the birth canal. By this time, I was so exhausted from pushing and in so much pain that I was vomiting with just about each contraction. I told the midwife that was it, I was done. I wanted a C-section. She feverishly tried to talk me out of my decision, blaming it on fatigue and my eagerness to see my baby. I remember my doula leaning in on my left side and trying to remind me of my birth plan. Back when I first began preparing for birth with my doula, one of the things we talked about was how she would know if I got to the "point of no return" and when she should step in and co-sign on any wacky requests I may make in the throws of labor. I told her not to worry, she would definitely know. Standing there next to me, she asked if I really wanted to go through all of that (c-section) after all of the work I had been doing and desire I had to be able to pull my baby boy out and into the world. I grabbed her hand and pulled it towards me and looked her wide-eyed in her face.

"Give me my fucking c-section!"

She quickly co-signed my request, as did the hubs. So it was settled. My all natural birth plan was completely out of the window and we waited the hour for our turn to go back to the operating room.

I don't know if it was due to my fear of operating rooms (as the patient) or just flat out exhaustion, but once the staff laid me on my back after administering my spinal block, I have absolutely no recollection of what came next. Nada. I remember nothing...not even hearing my baby boy's first cries. All I know is I woke up back in a different room than the one one I was originally in labor in. Almost immediately I felt so much pain in my lower abdomen. I let out a moan.

"How are you feeling, hun?" asked the nurse, standing at the right side of my bed keying information into the computer.

I replied *"I feel like a dinosaur kicked me in my back and out through my stomach."*

"Well, that's to be expected of someone who just had a c-section and a hysterectomy."

I was thrown off for a second by her response, and then I started looking around. I struggled to focus my eyes as I looked at the clock. It was 4am. I looked down at my hands and I had double IV's. The nurse noticed me looking at the second IV access in my other hand and explained that it was there because of the blood transfusion. WHAT?! I couldn't yell it because of the pain, but in my mind, that was what I screamed in disbelief. I guess she could see the shock in my face and she scrambled to gather her stuff together and said she would go and get my husband. He walked in a few seconds later and he had this look of shock mixed with fear in his face. He asked if I was okay.

"*Where's my baby?*" That's all I could say and that was all I wanted.

He ran out of the room and returned a few moments later, pushing a bassinet through the door. In that moment, all of my pain disappeared. He handed me a little swaddled up little bean. Mason Trevor was here. All 7lbs 9oz and 20 inches of a miracle was finally in my arms. I smelled him, snuggled him, and kissed him. I couldn't believe it. It was such a pure moment. I had to have this moment first, before I could address the elephant in the room. He couldn't tell me much because after the baby was born and "things started getting crazy and the doctor started screaming at people," he was taken out of the operating room with the baby to wait with the rest of the family in the birthing suite. Here I am, still in the dark about what led to me losing my uterus during my son's birth. A little while later, as I'm counting fingers and toes and inspecting every inch of my new little bundle of joy, the doctor comes back in the room to talk to me. He reassured me that everything went beautifully with Mason's birth ant that there were no complications at all. He further explained that once the baby was out and it was time to remove the placenta, I began to bleed out. He tried to control the bleeding, but couldn't because my placenta had grown into the wall of my uterus and there was no detaching it without bleeding to death--which was in progress...a condition called placenta accreta. So he was left with no other option but to take my uterus to keep me alive. He said that the entire time I was awake and responding to him--even when he told me about having to perform the hysterectomy. Marr also confirmed this. I have absolutely no knowledge of any of it. Thankfully, he opted to leave my eggs so that if I decided on more children in the future, I could have more via a surrogate. The doctor also commended me on my decision to listen to my body when I felt like I couldn't go any further with trying to push Mason out, because if I hadn't, he said that there wouldn't have been here to hold my baby. I was stunned. Here I am, happy and sad all at the same time. But the more I stared into the face of my perfect little miracle baby, the further back the sad was pushed. Thankful. That's all I could be.

After four days in the hospital, I was finally headed home with baby in tow. Well, baby and a barrage of medications. Pain meds because of the c-section, antibiotics and blood thinners because of the surgery, and blood pressure medications as a precaution to keep the pre-eclampsia at bay. I didn't care though. I was just happy to be going home. I quickly fell into a routine with the little guy. Heck, it wasn't hard to do, seeing as how I was the only one up and down with him. Thank goodness he was an easy baby. We were in a rhythm of wake up, nurse, smile and talk, then sleep. The first week had flown by.

I woke up on September 28th just like any other day as a mother of a newborn…tired. I had a little bit of a headache, but that was nothing uncommon or out of the ordinary. I got little man up, fed, changed, and back down for a nap, then took my medications as usual. Within about a half hour of him being asleep, I started feeling a little sick to my stomach. I attributed the nausea to the smell of the sausage that was being cooked in the kitchen at the time, and curled up in a ball in my bedroom waiting for it to be done. I quickly learned that the stinky sausage smell wasn't to blame when I took off running to the bathroom because of a sudden bout of diarrhea that I felt coming. I thought to myself, ok, maybe that's why I was nauseous…but things got worse, fast. After a few minutes of sitting on the toilet with an emesis bag full of puke and a toilet full of the trots, I felt incredibly weak. I could hardly sit up. I was out of breath. I was shaking and I was sweating. I felt it in my gut that something wasn't right and this wasn't just something that would go away. I managed to muster up enough breath to call for Marr and told him to call 911. He looked at me sitting on the toilet like, seriously?! You see, prior to me being pregnant, I had run rescue for a few years with the City of Virginia Beach. He knew how much I would harp about people calling 911 and tying up resources for minor ailments that could easily be addressed at an urgent care. But this wasn't that. I instructed him to tell the dispatcher that I was just a week postpartum and also post-op. I needed to make sure this was handled by a medic (as ALS) and not just as a basic sick call. When I told him all of that, I saw in his face that he realized this wasn't just me being dramatic.

The medic--who happened to be one of my favorites to run shifts with--arrived and saw me looking the hot mess that I felt. I remember hearing him say *"oh you look bad!"* He didn't waste any time getting me out the door and into the ambulance. Even though we've worked together for years, he very politely told me each little thing he was doing...asking if he could move my clothing to get an EKG and take my vitals. I reminded him that I already knew what had to be done and to just do it. That lightened the air, even if it were for only a moment. He took my blood pressure and it was insanely high. I'm talking like 200s over 100s. Shit got real! It wasn't even something I was expecting to see. I was rushed back to the labor and delivery department at the hospital that I had just delivered Mason. The staff that was on duty when I was wheeled in was actually the same staff that was on when I delivered and all remembered me. Everyone started pouring in and out of the room trying to figure out what was going on. While the registration tech was trying to get my info updated so that she could get my bracelet, yet another monkey wrench was thrown. While she was talking to me, it was getting harder and harder to speak and find my words to answer. She handed me the clipboard to sign the consent for treatment, but I couldn't grip the pen with my right hand to sign. I looked up and I saw the doctor's face. I already knew what was on her mind because it was on mine too, but I didn't want to get myself worked up and worsen the situation. Staff immediately shifted gears and within a matter of minutes, I was being wheeled down to CT to rule out a stroke. I was still nauseated, still lightheaded, still in pain, and scared out of my mind.

I had endured a magnesium drip, pleural effusion, and a slew of labs to manage my symptoms and to keep anything else from flaring up and causing problems. As it turns out, all of this was caused by postpartum preeclampsia--yet another rare situation. By the third day, I was finally well enough to be able to have my baby boy join me in my recovery room. All the while I was trying to recover, my main concern was with my kiddos, especially the newest of the bunch.

In a matter of two weeks, I had experienced two separate brushes with my mortality. Two different occasions that could have easily been ignored and had very different outcomes. Two different occasions where had I not listened to my gut and taken initiative to ensure I was truly okay, I very well may not be here today. They were then and are forever my strength. My kids fuel my will to live.

13

I CHOOSE ME

"Out of suffering have emerged the strongest souls; the most massive characters are seared with scars."
-Khalil Gibran

    I began the journey of writing this memoir back in the beginning of 2018. It was a time in my life where I felt like I hit a wall. HARD. My life was starting to feel like a rolling ball of chaos that I had absolutely no control over. To make matters worse, I wasn't happy. Now don't get me wrong...I am, have been, and always will be grateful for everything that I have and for having everything that I need. But there was this deep longing for something...something more. Well, some *things*. I didn't know what those "somethings" would be for quite some time, and to be completely transparent, I'm still learning what they are to this day. So, I tasked myself with writing this work and finishing it before 2019 rolled in. I knew going in that it was a major feat and one that I wasn't sure I could accomplish, but no sooner than those thoughts crossed my mind, did I immediately correct myself and my thinking. I've always been a person who lives to prove people wrong. Personal problem, I know! But when someone tells me I can't or expresses any form of doubt in me, it becomes my mission to prove that I am capable of doing anything I put my mind to. At times it can be a vice, but more often than not, it helps me to remember to have confidence in myself. Although I waited almost four years to finally publish, I am proud to say that I did accomplish my goal on December 30, 2018. I had something to be proud of. I also had something that helped me to discover voids in my life, as well as things and feelings that may still be unresolved...helping me to find those missing *things*.

One of the things that I felt almost a yearning to do was purge. **I needed to purge emotionally and mentally.** From about four years prior to the start of this writing journey, I had gone through a lot of big life moments that took a lot out of me. After I wrote what I thought was the entire project, a few more even bigger events took place that brought me to some pretty low places--lower than the bottom that I thought I had already reached. Usually, when I begin to feel overwhelmed, the beach was where I could go to have my own emotional enema. I had also gone to therapy for some time and that did help, to an extent. For me, I found that there was something more liberating in putting pen to paper and spilling my guts. I've never felt all the way comfortable talking about all of my issues, so I have the tendency to repress things for fear of being a burden on those I confide in. I guess you can say that's a byproduct of growing up in an environment where I didn't have the luxury of feeling like I was important, a priority, or feeling heard. Even being as close as I am with my closest friends. I still have a hard time giving up *everything* that I'm going through, but over time, I've learned that there are people in my life that I can trust. People who have my best interests at heart, and who do genuinely want to be there for me--in the difficult times and in the good times. It took some time, but I now realize that I had been holding on to all of the hurt and disappointment that I've experienced in my life from those that were *supposed* to be there for me unconditionally, and projecting an anticipation of disappointment on everyone I encounter. We learn from our experiences--which is a healthy reflex. We also have a tendency to go all in with trust in people, only to be hurt in the long run by some. But, what I have come to learn, accept, and practice is how to be vulnerable and allow those close to us in. It doesn't have to be all in right out of the gate...but little by little, until you discover whether or not a person is one you can trust and be completely open with. **If you shut everyone out, how will you know who you can let in and how will you ever learn to trust?**

This exercise of reflecting and writing has also helped me to see where and how I have lost myself over all of these years. Slowly but surely, it has helped me to find my voice, find myself, and learn to love me again. Growing up in a home where I was constantly stifled and wasn't able to share my feelings and truths really did have a major impact on my adult life. When I entered corporate America, I never hesitated to call out wrongdoings, injustices, and unfair treatment. That's just who I am. I would swiftly check disrespect, in a very corporate manner. I have the confidence and boldness to speak up when it was time to speak. Unfortunately, that would cause me to be mislabeled as the "angry black woman" and difficult to work with--only because I wouldn't tolerate mistreatment and lack of integrity. So as a reflex, I stifled myself. I filtered myself to appease bruised egos. I found myself living my childhood all over again. Then, I get married and its the same cycle. Stay stifled to keep the peace and avoid an argument, or be labeled as bitchy. I chose stifled. It took some time, but I discovered that choosing to keep the peace and appease egos created a war within me. I was relinquishing my own mental and emotional peace so that everyone else around me could be happy and comfortable. That had to stop, IMMEDIATELY. Now, when I find myself in a situation where I want to pull back to try and keep the peace, I take a moment to ponder if I am choosing to hurt myself to make someone else comfortable. Am I'm being accused of being aggressive simply because someone refuses to take ownership of their actions? Am I'm being called overbearing because someone is insecure? Or am I'm being called unfair by one who didn't get their way. If the answer to any of those questions is yes, then I choose to be an unapologetically intimidating go-getter. I refuse to dumb down or mute myself to pacify insecurities and stroke arrogant egos. I hold true and firm to my values, standards, and goals. **Don't be so understanding that you overlook the disrespect and the attempts to stifle your greatness.** That is now one of my golden rules.

Another thing that I have learned I needed to help me find "my happy" was time. I used to take pride in myself and the fact that I've literally had a job since I was 14 years old. From that time until I was 32 years old, I worked. And worked. And worked. I was never unemployed. This didn't become an issue for me until I became a parent.

Motherhood is the best thing that has ever happened to me, for a plethora of reasons. Among the most prominent though, is the change in perspective it provided me. We all know that becoming a parent changes your priorities from *me* to *my kids*. But for me, becoming a parent created a priority of what I can do, create, and leave for my children. As my children grew older and after years of early morning babysitter drop-offs, late evening babysitter pick-ups, and minimal hours of family time together care of my hectic work schedule and commute, I began to realize that I couldn't do anything for my kids if I was missing out on monumental moments. I couldn't create anything for them if I didn't have the energy at the end of the day to think from being exhausted after stressful days at work to even halfway function. I sure as hell couldn't leave them anything if I was living from paycheck to paycheck with nothing to show for it. I wanted to be there with and for my children. Something had to change, and it had to change fast!

It took a month of me crying every day I pulled into my parking spot at work and crying at the end of every shift before I finally decided to start making some moves. I wasn't one of those who was bold and brave enough to just make the decision to quit immediately and walk away from the consistency that I was so used to. I took baby steps. Hell, I had always said that I wouldn't ever just quit where I was working...and that they'd have to fire me to get me out of there so that I could collect my unemployment and take time to mentally decompress before jumping into anything new. Boy, do words have power!

I sat down one day and determined what it was that I wanted to do and how I would go about doing it. I began to use my time and my money wisely and laid the building blocks of what would be my own businesses. Something my children could grow into and eventually own on their own one day. I was proud of myself for what I was beginning to accomplish, but I was still miserable. Work was becoming increasingly toxic and it was getting really hard for me to resist just getting up and walking out each day. One Thursday in September, as I sat at my desk, a disgruntled employee, I received an email that would catapult me into my desires--quicker than I could have ever imagined.

As I sat at my desk doing my mundane work, I was sent an email from human resources that alleged I didn't follow supervisor instructions on three claims that were assigned to me--which was a hot lie! An offense of this type is cause for immediate termination. I don't play about the quality of my work and I don't play around when it comes to integrity, so this struck all of the wrong chords with me. As I read through the email in disbelief, I immediately began to formulate my rebuttal. These allegations were complete with claim numbers, date, and time stamps to supposed "instructions" that were documented by my supervisor that I was accused of ignoring. Needless to say, one of the first things I did was go into these files to see what it was I was being accused of ignoring. Are you ready for this? In all three...ALL THREE of the files that were cited in the notification from human resources, none of the instructions that I supposedly ignored existed. The whole accusation was false. It was all a lie cooked up by the supervisor that I was working for who did not care for me at all. My character and my integrity had been attacked for the last time. No doubt my response to the human resources manager was thorough and swift. As I left work that day, crying as usual on my way to my car, this small monarch butterfly fluttered next to my shoulder for about three or four parking spots, before flying away.

The next day, I returned to work to find that my situation had been escalated to the corporate human resources department for review and determination. I figured they would have my back and see that there was a deeper problem at hand here with this supervisor and her blatant fabrication, but Friday came and went without nary an update. I came in on Monday morning, eager for a response. I checked in with the department manager for a status update and she informed me that things were still under review. I remember telling her not to work me through the end of the day and then decide to let me go, because I'd be pissed and things would get ugly. Monday came and went, and towards the end of the work day, she let me know that there should be an update that following day. I was even more upset than I had been over those past few days. I had given this company so many of ny hours and so much of mine and my children's lives, and in return had been on the receiving end of so much mistreatment time and time again, then they had the audacity to do this?!

I came in on Tuesday morning, sat at my desk, unlocked my computer, and opened my Outlook and Messenger apps. I remember my supervisor coming by my desk and asking me why I hadn't checked my voicemails yet or started taking any calls. I calmly and politely told her that I would start my work day once I found out if I still worked there or not. Within 30 minutes, my inbox dinged. It was my manager requesting me to come to her office. It was all over. I was officially fired for a lie. Fuming doesn't even begin to describe how angry I was. I snatched my termination envelope out of her hand, swiped by badge for the last time, and left. But then it hit me and I heard:

"Why are you fighting this so hard? I'm giving you exactly what you asked for."

You see, I was so wrapped up and distracted by the disrespect I felt, that I was completely missing the blessing of the whole situation. I was so afraid to take the leap of faith and leave the job that I'd known for so long to start my own, that God had to literally stretch his foot down from the heavens and kick me out the door. I was so worked up about how my name was being smeared and what people would think, that I wasn't looking ahead to the fact that this fabricated termination didn't hold up--which meant that I would be entitled to my unemployment AND the little bit of pension that I had accrued while I was there. All of these events have allowed me to be at home with my children since 2015. For the first time in their lives, I was able to have breakfast with them, take them to school, be there when they got home, help them with homework, and get things done while they were at school so that when they got home we could spend quality time together. Financially, I was able to take care of obligations without worry or doubt, and I was even able to fully launch and invest in my businesses. I was finally able to *can* and *create* for my seed. As I walked up my lawn from taking the kids to school for the first time, a giant monarch butterfly flew around ahead of me and then off towards the treetops. Right then, I knew for sure for sure that things were going to be just fine.

> *"For I know the plans I have for you, declares the Lord, plans for welfare and not for evil, to give you a future and a hope."*
> – Jeremiah 29:11
>
> *"And we know that in all things God works for the good of those who love him, who have been called according to his purpose."*
> – Romans 8:28

The process of finding yourself again after so many negative experiences is no easy feat. It doesn't happen quickly. This process requires you to commit to ripping off the Band-Aids of past hurts, acknowledging triggers and figuring out how you'll work through those hurts when they present themselves in various forms throughout your lifetime. It also requires you to follow through on the promises you make to yourself to be the best version of you that you can be. *That's* the hard part. That's usually where we end up bargaining and diminishing ourselves for the sake of others. It's at that junction that you have to remind yourself that you can't pour from an empty cup. Finding yourself is a form of self care, and self care is key! Finding myself and my happy takes a daily commitment from me to remember that while everything in life ebbs and flows, I'm going to continue to remain true to me and hold on to my confidence. Each day comes with highs and lows, but I have to make the conscious decision and effort to climb up out of those lows and celebrate the highs.

Even if its by myself, I choose me and I choose to dance.

ACKNOWLEDGEMENTS

"Surround yourself with people who add value to your life. Who challenge you to be greater than you were yesterday. Who sprinkle magic into your existence, just like you do to theirs. Life isn't meant to be done alone. Find your tribe, and journey freely and loyally together."
-Alex Elle

Over the years, my girlfriends have become my sounding boards, my home, and most importantly my family. Some have come and gone, but there are a few who have stood the test of time. I don't have a circle of friends like most. My circle is so small, its practically a dot. I proudly call these women members of my dot. They are my sisters. My heartbeats. They get me and I get them. We have our spats, but we put petty to the side and don't let misunderstandings get in the way of friendship. We tell each other what we need to hear when we need to hear it, never with contempt or malice. In my book, that's what a true friend is. *This* is a tribe. Kiya, Nicole, Monica, Stacy, Shaquey, Nicholette, Sam...these women have been key players in the major moments and events in my life, and I am so glad God placed them in my path.

I thank you: Kiya, Nicole, Monica, Stacy, Shaquey, Nicholette, Sam, and also Tanesha, Liz, Toot, Aunt Candi, and Aunt Diane for being the judgement free zone that I could rely on and vent to when times get tough—and for keeping all of our family dirt swept under the rug—until I was ready to spill all the tea.

You ladies are my rocks.

Forever and always.